# About the

Mark Ritchie is a familiar nar
on the inside of the light en
Clubland and the holiday park entertainment
scene in the UK, as well as in what remains of UK
variety.

A media pundit as well as a singer and stand-up
comedian, Mark has never been a household name,
but his time working for *The Stage* newspaper and
in the local press and on various radio projects over
many years in his native Yorkshire, has kept Mark's
profile high.

His autobiography, *Right Place... Wrong Time*
(published October 2020) is his amusing yet also
deeply moving account of a life which saw Mark
serving in so many lines of work. These included a
spell in the police force and the DIY business He
also spent working down a Yorkshire coal mine,
before going out and learning his craft in the tough
Yorkshire working men's clubs, where he has been
renowned for many years as an in-demand
comedian who also possesses a great singing voice.

Mark's showreel can be seen on his website at
www.mark-ritchie.co.uk. His lengthy CV is also
available on the site.

Now married to his second wife Beverley, Mark
has two grown-up children from his first marriage,
as well as a number of grandchildren.

Mark lives quietly in a rather remote country
village not too far from Wakefield in West Yorkshire, with Beverley and their two beloved Old
English sheepdogs Stan and Ollie.

# THE CLUBLAND EMPIRE

## My Part in Its Downfall

Mark Ritchie

DESERT♥HEARTS

First published
in 2022 by
**DESERT♥HEARTS**
www.deserthearts.com

www.mark-ritchie.co.uk

www.ukcabaret.com

© Mark Ritchie 2022

Typeset and designed by Desert♥Hearts

Printed and bound in Great Britain by
Printforce

British Library Cataloguing in Publication Data
A catalogue record for this book is available from the British Library

ISBN 9781908755520

**

Every effort has been made to contact and obtain
permission from owners of copyrighted material
included in this book. In case of oversight
please contact the publishers.

*This book is respectfully dedicated to all those entertainers and musicians who remember the fun we all had during the great days of Clubland and all of us who perhaps foolishly remained on the scene for far too long, only to watch it all unravel before our very eyes. The patient has lost so much of its lifeblood and is now on life-support. The turning off of the switch can't be far away now, as we finally put the Clubland patient out of its misery.*

# Contents

# Introduction

Most readers of my autobiography *Right Place... Wrong Time* seemed to agree on the view expressed at the time by my wife, that the most interesting stories I can tell are those concerning the oddly fractured yet sometimes exciting life I have led. When a second book was decided upon, I knew immediately that this volume would not simply consist of untold stories left over from book number one. I had other ideas.

What I am offering here is an insight into a mode of living which seems to be fading away fast from 21st century society. Largely forgotten already by many and with the effects of the Covid-19 pandemic possibly putting the tin lid on the whole outmoded concept of 'Club Life', I am writing here about a lifetime spent working in one capacity or another in the field of the great British working men's club movement.

So we will begin at the beginning by remembering how at all began, before quickly moving on to the heydays of the 1970s when I first became involved as a member of my own local club.

After writing columns, features and reviews for so

many years and visiting so many club venues across the land for so long in my capacity as a jobbing entertainer, I suddenly began to consider putting both my life and my stories from the club scene into book form.

I first began to make notes for a possible book while I was on honeymoon with my second wife, who I always refer to as 'My Bevvy'. Her name is Beverley. She likes to be called Bev. I like to call her Bevvy.

It was 2011 and we were on a tiny island in the Indian Ocean called Hudhuranfushi, which is one of the many hundreds of small patches of sand and rock which collectively make up the Maldives Islands. These many hundreds of low-lying islands and islets straddle the Equator and look like no other place on Earth I have ever visited before or since. While on the island I took a huge note pad with me and started jotting.

I was unaware of the fact that I was ill at that time. As it turned out I was very ill indeed. After being rendered unconscious one evening by an uncontrollable coughing fit, I was taken to the doctor's surgery, which turned out to be a breeze-block hut on the beach, complete with a tin roof. A chest infection was diagnosed, antibiotics were administered and I was kept quiet and largely secluded in our luxury accommodation, which stood out in the sea on stilts and which was known rather grandly as an Ocean Villa. To pass the time I began to write, write and then write some more.

The stories from my life began to spew out like a fractured sewage pipe and I soon realised that while I could crack on with the autobiography, the book about the clubs would have to be put on the back-burner. I started on the first book, but the most perplexing question was whether anyone actually want to read it? Even if I was fortunate enough to become a published author at the time, I knew that I could never publish the full story while my parents were alive. For those who haven't yet read my autobiography, if you take a look at the volume in some detail, you are sure to appreciate why.

We travelled home from the Indian Ocean and the cough, which my GP had been treating for many weeks previously as acid reflux, had developed into pneumonia. After our return to the UK the illness still remained undiagnosed due to a cock-up in the X-ray department at my local hospital. The pneumonia fluid eventually formed an abscess in one of my lungs, which burst bang on cue right in time for Christmas. I was admitted to hospital and spent the entire festive period in the intensive care unit fighting for my life. Once recovering, I spent most of my time watching movies on a portable DVD-player, but also making more notes towards telling the stories which eventually were told in my autobiography and are now detailed within the pages of this book too.

In the summer of 2016, I was diagnosed with a condition called post-traumatic stress disorder. I found the task of dealing with a severe mental illness rather daunting. As a consequence of being categorised as being officially bonkers and with not much in the way of meaningful work coming my way, I found myself strolling up and down the surprisingly cheery corridors of the Fieldhead psychiatric hospital in my native Wakefield, Yorkshire.

My skewed perception of the whole mental illness experience was that it all seemed deeply shaming. Part of my survival strategy was to hold on tightly to what I knew to be real and true and try to eschew what then seemed like the very real option of hurting myself and my almost overwhelming desire to hurt certain other people, who had behaved despicably toward me for reasons best known to themselves. In short, I was in a mess.

Puzzled and perplexed by what turned out to be my misapprehension that only battle-weary soldiers could be labelled as suffering from PTSD and convinced I had been misdiagnosed, I trotted along to my first regular appointment with the kindly and knowledgeable 'shrink' I had been assigned to.

"Call me Fiona!" was my psychiatrist's welcoming instruction and soon we were occupying a small office-type consulting room for a long series of regular appointments which culminated in EMDR therapy, an odd kind of treatment involving a rapid eye-movement technique which was new to the UK then. I'm pretty sure this treatment saved my life. I'm told that five years on from when I first accepted the treatment, EMDR is now an integral weapon in the treatment of PTSD.

I was hanging on to my sanity by my fingertips, as if dangling from a very tall building. My choice was to either let go and fall to what I then regarded as the peace and comfort of my own death, or reset, refocus and readjust to finding out new things about the fractured and frenetic life I had been leading. During this nadir within what was a truly chaotic period, the whole battle to regain my sanity was lengthy and a hard, hard slog. My writing certainly helped and some of my jottings from that time appear now in this written effort, where I attempt to explain where it all went so wrong for the once glorious Clubland I had grown up indoctrinated into the ways of as a child.

In between writing 'splurges', my anxiety levels were off the scale. I would spend long periods battling imaginary attackers, both asleep and while awake. The nightmares were horrendous. Bevvy began to recognise the signs, and her love and care were key to the beginning of my recovery. I couldn't actually feel emotion or pain at all sometimes and I began to self-harm. I also used to drive too fast, but only on quiet motorways at night. Sleep was erratic, spasmodic or non-existent, and sometimes the pills just didn't work. Instead, for hours and even full nights I would sit up and focus on getting all my Clubland stories down on paper.

I was encouraged to focus on interests which could absorb my complete attention, if only for a while. My new friend and mentor figure 'Call-Me-Fiona' advised that I needed a safe place to go back to in my head and even a physical safe location, where I could reflect and regroup my thoughts and feelings. In order to divert my mind away from my preconceived ideas and perceptions in regard to life as an outpatient at the local psychiatric hospital, I was determined to rekindle interest in past hobbies. Aided greatly by my Old English sheepdog Oscar, who focused my mind on his unconditional friendship and love, as well as making me laugh a lot, I began the long road back.

Ignoring strict doctor's orders, I continued performing on Clubland and holiday park stages up and down the country, mainly in one-nighters. I found that whilst battling a mental health breakdown, going onstage was easy. I could become someone else for a while and accentuate the positive by making people laugh. The only caveat in my willingness to appear in live cabaret was that I would seldom speak closely to anyone about my performances either on or after each show.

I kept out of everyone's way, which determined that I managed to avoid the fatuous platitudes and well-meaning bouquets from admirers and the occasionally nasty brickbats from those with either no sense of humour or some other point to prove.

Aside from Bevvy, few people outside of the psychiatric hospital knew about any of the mental health problems I was tussling with. Until I thought the time was right to start talking, I maintained my silence and withdrew from much of the world I once thought I knew.

The deep irony was that some of the work coming my way at this time was from a most unlikely source. Two of the people who had accelerated my mental illness by their duplicity and dishonesty were coming up with stage work and giving patronage to a new magazine publishing project I had launched at that time. I like to think there may have been just a tiny shred of decency in these truly horrid individuals and this was part of their guilt trip. Finally, this gruesome twosome eventually seemed to overcome their pricking consciences and soon turned the financial tap off, once it became clear they had been rumbled and they discovered that I had known about their ulterior motives for a very long time.

For the devious and dishonest, being seen through must be the hardest part of being a complete bastard and surely remains at the back of their minds for years. Who knows, perhaps that is their penance and a price they have to pay for their greed and duplicity.

Many people may consider that carrying on in business and working my way through all of this, when I had come within an ace of being sectioned under the Mental Health Act, was foolhardy. But keeping busy was part of my survival strategy and in the end, this turned out to be my salvation. I was proved right, but I just had to do it my own way. I quickly learned that by using a subtle form of obfuscation, I could deflect my limited attention span away from any undue fixation on my perilous financial situation. As I have already mentioned, my penury was deliberately created by others, due to a series of bizarre business problems which involved some very nasty, avaricious and vindictive people.

My mind had to be filled with anything and everything I found absorbing. It was sink or swim. I researched my family history, and I also believe I may well have solved the mystery of the so-called Jack the Ripper murders, which took place in East London and began in the late summer of 1888.

At the time of writing this introduction, I have just returned from a stay in the East End of London, where I continued my research into the whole three-ring circus that has been created by the many thousands of people worldwide, dubbed 'Ripperologists'. From my hotel close to Aldgate East tube station, I wandered the streets where Jack the Ripper struck, or at least what remains of them. The area is now 'upwardly mobile', with a giant shopping complex in the planning stages in an area of Brick Lane, which comes up time and time again for those looking to establish the identity of the serial killer who was dubbed 'Jack the Ripper' by the tabloid press of the day.

Overlay maps are necessary now to see how original buildings and street scenes looked then, in comparison to now in 21st-century London. I think I can prove beyond all reasonable doubt that there were three men involved, either directly or indirectly, in the murders during which I believe eleven women died between 1888 and 1891.

The man supplying the motive for some of the murders was an American quack doctor called Francis Tumblety. His body is interred in a cemetery in Rochester, New York State in America. I believe that a known associate of Tumblety by the name of Walter Thomas Porriott was an accomplice for at least four of the murders. I visited Porriott's grave some years ago in Brisbane, Australia. Furthermore, I believe that I may be able to prove conclusively that Jack the Ripper himself worked as a mortuary attendant in Whitechapel. His name was Robert Mann.

My lifetime fascination with the murders, for which

no one was ever convicted, has proved many things to me. First and foremost, that once armchair sleuths have decided on their chosen suspect, they seldom switch allegiances, sticking doggedly with their own perceptions of what constitutes solid and irrefutable proof.

As I said earlier the use of maps and then and now style photography took me in the direction of what is now a GLC-built housing estate, erected during the 1970s. There was a lucky chance meeting with a historian from University College London, who told me he was living in the former Davenant church, and a friendly postman put me right on the site of what was the original workplace of Robert Mann, situated in what used to be Eagle Place, Whitechapel.

By pacing out the distance between where the Whitechapel Workhouse Infirmary once stood, and where Robert Mann slept, and the site formerly occupied by the mortuary, which stood where Eagle Place used to be, I estimate it would have taken Robert Mann about ninety seconds to walk from his bed at the infirmary to the mortuary. At least some of his victims were taken to the same mortuary and there is documentary proof that he himself prepared the victims for post-mortem. His anatomical knowledge came from literally standing at the elbow of the coroner/doctor as he worked. The mortuary provided jars and preservatives in which I believe Mann kept some of the victim's organs and also provided a secure hiding place for him on the nights of the attacks. Conceivably he could also use the privacy the small mortuary premises afforded to change clothing and suddenly disappear from view. As Mann held the keys to the mortuary, which stood close to Old Montague Street right in the heart of the killing zone, he could hide in plain sight as a well-known person with a genuine reason to be exactly where he was at any given time.

I plan another book, which I hope will be successful, in which I present all my research to what is sure to be a sceptical bunch of Ripperologists and a more open-minded majority of potential readers. I have even discovered a solid link between the Victorian Queen of the Music Halls Marie Lloyd and the Jack the Ripper murders. Perhaps I will present the next book with the title *Showbusiness and Jack the Ripper*?

Busy fingers are happy fingers!

As the Covid-19 global nightmare began in spring 2020, I set about the ultimate act of self-indulgence by pushing on with the act of getting my autobiography *Right Place... Wrong Time* down on paper. 65,000 words later, the book was published by a long-time friend and colleague and to my astonishment it sold oodles of copies. The sales orders are still trickling in. The whole experience of getting so much of my life down on paper and into book form proved exactly the cathartic exercise I had hoped it would be.

By March 2021, it then seemed the right time to begin something new. The title of this book may seem puzzling. When I was a young lad, I was given a selection of books as a present. The great Spike Milligan was the author and I loved reading his stories and verse. His war memoirs were entitled *Adolf Hitler: My Part in His Downfall.*

Milligan used his accustomed irony, witty and caustic descriptive powers to delve into his time as a soldier and the true extent of the 'contribution' he and his comrades made to the fall of the Nazis.

I suppose here I am trying to use the same kind of irony to chart my time involved in a movement which has been in decline for the entire span of what I laughingly refer to as my career. Whilst making a handsome living for many years, I have watched the business we once called 'show' slowly but inexorably disintegrating before my very eyes.

As I mentioned I have a staunch ally and supportive publisher in Nick Awde at Desert Hearts. Whilst pulling the business strings, I know Nick was keen from the beginning on a further book, involving even more revelations from this bizarre half-life in show business and elsewhere in which I have lived.

In many ways it started long before I was born. At various periods of their lives, my parents and grandparents were all involved in what was once known as 'Club Life'. My maternal grandfather was a well-known singer and he and my grandmother also worked as club stewards, running and maintaining a once busy social club in Wakefield, Yorkshire, which like so many thousands of others has now gone forever.

Here I can write not only about my life but the lives of so many more – or many less – gifted entertainers who all found there was a good living to be earned on the stages of working men's clubs, community clubs, political clubs, works social clubs, masonic halls, holiday camps and even church-based social clubs, so many of which once existed the length and breadth of this Island Nation. Many venues still remain but it's just not the same somehow.

My dad was a part-time club singer and a full-time coal-miner. My mother was a pianist and organist who worked the clubs as a backing musician, as well as serving as pianist and accompanist for my grandad, who was known professionally as 'Whistling Ted Marlowe'. He was a great tenor singer and he died when I was 21. I loved him very much and I was only sorry he did not live long enough to see me making a living on Clubland stages as a singer and comedian. I hope I would have made him proud.

The club and institute movement itself began in early Victorian times, but this book will focus in the main on first-hand accounts from the period in which I began in Clubland during the 1970s.

By that time Clubland meant shows and live music and entertainment. These were the heydays of the clubs and my story will continue right through to the present day, as live entertainment venue numbers continue to plummet and the whole scene edges ever more closely towards oblivion.

Soon the whole concept of what I refer to here as 'Clubland' (the working men's clubs or WMC scene) will be consigned to the dustbin of history. The world moves on and the only people who become rich within the leisure market are those with the nous and foresight to spot what exactly the next 'big thing' will be. I myself have no idea, but for someone who has never been really good at anything much in life, the club sector and other sectors of show business I have worked in have provided me with a good living for many a long year and from that I derive much satisfaction.

A combination of profligacy, speculation and sheer bad judgement had left me virtually skint at the age of 62, after having earned so much money over so many years. Hey-ho! That is the life I have led and it is way too late in the day for regrets. Without the aid of a crystal ball, I could not possibly have foreseen the extraordinary set of circumstances which I revealed only last year in my autobiography.

Now, if you are good and kind enough to make the modest investment required to buy a copy of this book, thank you. If your local club and the acts, performers and bands that you remember are not featured within these pages, I can only apologise. The names and places which live in your memory are just as much a part of the great Clubland story as any recollections and reminiscences of my own.

Additionally, an integral part of what I also want to examine and highlight in this book is how and why the working men's clubs became such a key factor within the everyday lives of hard-working people from the old heavy industrial communities.

Now a pale shadow of the huge business it all once was, I have tapped into my own bank of memories and raided those of others, in order to enjoy our Clubland tales from the past. Sadly, I cannot avoid or disagree with the collective view held and expressed by so many other

Clubland insiders that the remaining community clubs across the UK haven't a snowball's chance in hell of maintaining any conceivable long-term possibility of any kind of a viable business future.

While our memories of the days when Clubland was so pivotal in all our lives and communities, remain largely intact and while we can still bathe in sentimentality, as we recollect a time when people worked together, lived together and played together, it is time to tell all. Or at least all that I can remember of my own involvement within this singularly peculiar sector of the UK leisure market.

The tapestry of Clubland is surprisingly broader than the uninformed and uninitiated may realise. This is a huge story, so please be patient with me as I scratch the surface of the great Clubland entertainment story and inform those too young to know what Clubland was all about and just how important the scene was in the lives of so many.

The old communities, described for so long politically as the 'Red Wall', are now neglected and under-represented. Many of them have even gone Tory – so ironic as the inhabitants of the communities decimated by Thatcherism in the 1980s are now represented by the public-school educated disciples of the Iron Lady herself. In the view of so many us of disenfranchised ex-Labour members and voters, the Labour Party does not exist today as an effective opposition. In the view of many political commentators, it will take a generation to recover from decisions taken during Brexit and the existence of the student-heavy, politico-loving party within the party-political death cult which we know as Momentum.

Labour MPs have 'form' in the whole field of forgetting their responsibilities to constituents which they took on once elected. Following a rigid code or dogma is exactly how the similarly destructive Militant tendency formed in the 1980s. As a former party activist myself, I fought and played a very small role in booting Militant out of Labour. I am too old and weak now to rejoin the fight for social justice, which I and so many others from my generation believed just had to be fought back then.

The Red Wall members of parliament blundered along between 2016 and 2019, blindly ignoring the vast majority of those of us who put them in power, by virtue of the prism through which they viewed Europe. Instead of reflecting the views of the vast majority of their constituents, as they are paid so handsomely to do, they simply demonstrated their slavish devotion to Europe and the corrupt and undemocratic EU, up until and including the 2019 election, by attempting to block the whole Brexit process. So many of them lost their seats due to their own arrogance and complacency and I say good riddance to bad rubbish.

Although my past involvement as a Labour party activist and official was quite small in terms of making any kind of meaningful contribution, nevertheless I was a coal miner during the Great Strike of 1984/85 and I witnessed and felt the effects of the dispute first hand. In the hope that some of today's bright young things may learn more about the roots of the party and its influence in the local working-class communities of yesteryear, I will tell the stories once again, including the integral part played in the struggle by the local clubs and the miners' welfare schemes.

The old heavy industries were dismantled and aren't coming back any time soon. The people who now live in these communities don't seem to recognise the importance of social cohesion and a sense of community pride. Generally speaking, they don't go to the high street, they shop online. They don't socialise, they stay in and watch Sky TV. They don't engage with their neighbours, they live in their own bubble, with so many vegetating as their brains turn to 21st-century mush. As people mill around in their all-day everyday cocoons, I recall reading Orwell as a boy and the world that seems so bleak, humourless and monochrome today makes me realise how Winston must have felt in *1984*.

My intention in the pages which follow are to provide a taste of the atmosphere within the communities I grew up in. We can also take a stroll down memory lane and remember the whole Clubland experience and what it was like to see a Clubland show or become a club member. I hope to illustrate the sheer anticipation of a great Clubland night out, seeing our mates, enjoying good beer and celebrating our brotherhood, sisterhood and sense of neighbourhood.

We have a lot of ground to cover, so let's get to it!

*

# 1
# Club life...
# how it began

The Reverend Henry Solly was full of good intentions. A temperance minister and social reformer admired by welfare state architect William Beveridge no less, Solly wanted to curb excessive drinking and instead channel the focus and energy of working men into more wholesome and educational pursuits. Solly stated such local clubs could address the social ills of 'intemperance, ignorance, improvidence and religious indifference'.

Solly quickly attracted interest and support from his large network of wealthy and influential friends. The only cloud on the horizon – from Solly's point of view at least – was that those who rolled out the financial support and patronage didn't all hold the same views on the evils of alcoholic consumption and excess.

The problem was that consuming alcohol was always synonymous with the concept of socialising. Alehouses, gin houses, taverns and other public houses catered for the need and in some cases the addictions of their customers. Within the inner cities and the slums of everyday life, many people drank to blot out or at least diminish too much thought on the horrors of what their everyday lives consisted of. A manual worker could end his shift, head for the pub and drink lots of beer every day, which would be sweated out of his pores again the following working day and so on and so forth.

Solly was far from alone amongst Victorian churchmen in the wish to see young lads engaged in more fruitful activities during their leisure time. In Yorkshire, around the area I grew up in, there was the Reverend Tiverton Preedy. Soon after moving into his parish in Barnsley, the reverend managed to garner support from the local business community to form a local football club. Lots of young lads, who spent their working lives down Victorian coal mines came along to fields that Preedy had managed to obtain use of from a local cooperative society. The Barnsley St Peter's football club was formed and clearly boasted pretty good facilities which attracted the best players in the area. Elected to the football league in 1887, the club went on to be known simply as Barnsley football club and even went on to win the FA Cup in 1912.

Just over 20 years ago, the club of which I am a lifelong supporter of, went into administration and that could very well have been the end, until a local computer software magnate called Patrick Cryne came in, bought the club for £1, thereby accepting responsibility for the debts for £20 million which had accrued. Cryne saved Barnsley FC from going under and, soon after, the club invested in a set of giant flags emblazoned with the faces of Cryne and Preedy. The text on the flag read 'One Made Us – One Saved Us'.

Cryne succumbed to a long battle with cancer a few years ago. I knew him slightly and, like Solly and Preedy before him, he too was full of good intentions. When Cryne sold the club to the international consortium who own it now, all he asked for was his £20 million back. A group of fans of Barnsley FC still travel to London every year to attend to the grave of the Reverend Preedy.

Meanwhile back in Victorian England, Solly opened clubs firstly in the London area which were free from intoxicating liquor and which presented opportunities for learning and self-improvement. One Haringey club supporter at the time defined a working men's club in this way:

> "A club is a coming together of like-minded individuals for common purposes, be they social, educational, recreational or political."

According to Solly himself, a club should offer good companionship and educational activities, but with no profits for breweries and publicans. The good reverend also went on to opine that clubs should offer light refreshments only. Some individual landowners set up social clubs for farmhands and tenants, but they were very different set-ups to WMCs as they did not belong to their own members.

The historian Peter Bailey once described working

men's clubs as "the most prominent example of rational recreation formally organised on a national scale". They were seen by many well-intentioned people as a compromise. On the one hand they provided meeting places for working men, but without the beer. The Salvation Army, supported by temperance campaigners were very active in the big cities, with reports of many during the 1850s and 60s marching into pubs, all armed with bibles and singing hymns as they tried to provide patrons with an opportunity to sign 'the pledge'. Indeed, helping the existence of the early clubs was the very thought of the alternative, which largely consisted of being preached at inside a cold church hall while sipping tea. Clubs could exist in order to provide a safe, warm and welcoming place without the preaching – but also without the beer.

So many of the Charles Dickens books describe, often in graphic detail, the grim living conditions in the Victorian inner-city slums. Many of the single men living in lodgings were allowed only to sleep where they lodged and were sent out onto the streets when not working. The choices were heading off for tea and sympathy in church, going to the pub and spending hard-earned money on beer, or joining a local club and getting away from the hassle of everyday life.

For women there was no choice, as they were considered there simply to procreate with and subsequently to look after the children that appeared. However incommodious and cramped the living conditions were, the women just had to get on with their lives. During my own life and times spent in the clubs, women were still not permitted to be members of most clubs, and in the clubs they were actually allowed to venture into, there were often rooms they were not allowed to enter, as they were designated 'men only'.

During the early 1860s, the clubs were getting their collective act together by forming the C&IU. The Club and Institute Union was designed to offer practical help and advice to fledgling clubs in the hope of seeing them develop within their own local community. At first this union consisted of just six clubs in the London area, including Bethnal Green WMC, which is still open today. The numbers grew quickly as word of the movement spread across the country and in 1864 the clubs were brought under the cover of 'The Friendly Societies Act', which saw them all drawing up annual financial statements.

Solly's list of supporters was filled with celebrities of the day, including the politician Lord Rosebery who expressed his view that the clubs should be run by working men themselves and not, as he put it at the time "being patronised by benefactors". In fact, a special general meeting of the C&IU in 1886 determined that the clubs should be run by elected members from within their own ranks. A trade unionist called B. T. Hall was elected C&IU general secretary in 1893 – coming from a working-class background, he proved a popular choice and remained in the post until 1929.

As the C&IU reach expanded, it began to open area branches of the union, which saw the first appearing in

Wiltshire in 1894. Membership fees were introduced and this is how individual clubs started to fund the C&IU. This meant there was no further reliance of gifts and donations, which had been accepted as the norm before.

Henry Solly died in 1903 and while he and others faded into the background, the numbers of clubs joining what became known as 'The Union' was mushrooming. Many smaller communities saw clubs starting up. My own great grandfather Joe White helped start a club in the village of Ryhill in Yorkshire around 1896.

Joe was the club's first treasurer and the premises, which remain standing and in business today, was called Ryhill WMC. Maybe the club has almost turned full-circle as this club (now known as Ryhill village club, is owned and operated by a fairly reclusive brewery magnate and property developer who runs the Sam Smith's brewery in Tadcaster near York. Part of the Smith brewing dynasty, the latest Mr Smith does not allow any form of music, swearing, television or even mobile phones into any of his pubs and clubs, which in my view basically means he is trying to turn back the clock and make clubs places of education and friendship while shutting the rest of the world out.

The big cities had their distractions, but in the towns and smaller communities the club became a focal point of contact for men of all ages in the community. Club rule books had to be adhered to very closely as the desire for respectability was strong. Those running clubs did not want to throw themselves open to criticism from outsiders or claims that clubs were simply self-regulating public houses, still barely tolerated by theologians and lifetime alcohol-abstainers.

The C&IU did not issue edicts or try and impose their will on those running individual clubs. Instead, they distributed advice and what C&IU general secretary Hall once referred to as "sensible guidelines", which stated that club premises should be brighter and cheerier than most which may be found in the homes of club members.

Typically, early club premises consisted of rented space above shops, in which men could be found gathering in a reading room, as many men could not afford newspapers and books. There would most probably be men gathered around tables, playing cards, dominos or cribbage. As the clubs grew, so did the facilities they offered, with skittles and even billiard tables being added.

The scene was now set for the development of an entire strand of UK social history, which would become vast and peak during the early 1970s with over 4,500 individual clubs operating within the UK, the majority of which would be offering at least some form of live entertainment.

Clubland benefited hugely from the death of the variety theatre circuit, of that there is no doubt whatsoever. While variety was still going through its death throes, the huge numbers of touring acts turned to the burgeoning club scene of the early 1970s to find alternative employment. By then many of the bigger clubs were offering week-long engagements and even residencies. In addition to all of this, the cabaret career path was further reinforced as the bigger and glitzier variety clubs were well established by this time and providing the opportunities for club-goers to see their favourite television stars of the day.

After post-war austerity, people were dining out and looking for the best in live entertainment. Autograph hunting and even having photos taken with the stars was common. This was boom time.

\*

# 2

# The Clubland family

Before I arrive at my own first appearance on a Clubland stage and my early involvement in other Clubland roles, I should colour the backstory of my Clubland journey.

It was 1945 and my father was 18 on January 12th of that year. The Germans were retreating, the Allies were advancing into Germany and the Nazi gangsters were sinking ship-rats, all getting as far away from their deeds as possible with some even hoping for the start of a Fourth Reich in Argentina.

In 1941 my father started work underground down Monckton colliery. I remember 40 years later, during our 'snap-time', or meal break, Dad and I were perched atop a huge electrical transformer, eating sandwiches. We were around 450 metres underground, deep in the bowels of the earth, down Nostell colliery where we were both employed at the time.

Dad was a proper pitman plying a proper mines

mechanics-type trade, which was that of a rope-splicer.
I was just trying to find my way and make some leeway
in life, which was pretty much impossible as I was simply
a square peg in a round hole.

The pit we worked down was situated near Wakefield
in Yorkshire. Nostell colliery was cold and wet, and the
transformer Dad and I were both perched upon that day
was warm and helping to dry our clothes. We had
become wet as I just finished helping Dad to dig out part
of a piece of machinery called a return wheel. As a rope
splicer, Dad was very much in charge – I was employed
to do another job, but my shift had ended and he saw me
heading towards the pit bottom and the twice-daily ride
in the 'cage', the elevator that would take me and all my
workmates back to the surface.

Dad had arranged for some overtime and had
requested me to help him. Our pit bags had been filled
with sandwiches, which had been sent down the pit and
brought to us. We chose to try and dry off and eat at the
same time in our cosy underground nook. The place was
full of rodents which would eat anything in sight if given
half a chance, so we unhooked our bags, which contained
our lunch, from pieces of metal which were attached to
the roof supports, well out of reach of the multitude of
blind creatures that lived in the all-enveloping darkness
and which crawled around below us.

I could feel one of Dad's stories coming on and soon
he was reminiscing about 1945 and the day he became a
member of Ryhill Liberal club. A political club in name
only and known locally as 'The Lib', I don't suppose there

were many supporters of the then soon-to-be Liberal prime minister David Lloyd George when the club was formed in 1909 by a local dentist, Mr Dunleavy.

My grandfather Albert Webster Goodwin was already a member of the club and Dad was proposed for membership of the club by his uncle Wilf Kinch and seconded by his friend Hubert Normington. Dad did a bit of boxing at a gymnasium in nearby Royston, but his main interest was singing in a local choir and dreaming of going on the stage. Armed with a useful baritone, Dad and his friends – the aforementioned Mr Normington and another friend and neighbour called Colin Rasen – were village lads all blessed with an ear for a tune and aspirations of stardom.

Post-war austerity meant rationing and most of the clubs within the pit villages made their own entertainment, with piano singalongs the order of the day. By then the clubs were just beginning to look to the future, but the then booming variety theatre was the real target for all aspiring entertainers.

Dad's problem was that all he knew was the pit, where he began in 1941 by doing the job all young boys were assigned to, with the intention of making them become accustomed to spending long dark hours underground. He was engaged in opening and closing air doors, as the hard-working pit ponies approached, tugging their heavy loads of machinery or coal. Eventually many of the boys, including Dad, were engaged as pony drivers. The horses lived, ate and slept underground in specially built stables. At regular intervals they were transported up the pit shafts and allowed to gambol and chew the sweet grass of the fields in the fresh air above.

During our snap-time story time in 1981, Dad told me about the ponies and about one particular animal who toiled down Monckton colliery, the pit Dad worked at before being transferred to nearby Nostell Colliery in 1966. Other boys worked alternative shifts and one morning Dad found some horrendous marks on the body of the pony known as Dick. Asking around, Dad discovered that a lad who he knew well was responsible for the animal's maltreatment. My father asked him nicely to stop what he was doing, which didn't work. The subsequent fight was long and bloody, but suffice it to say the pony was never harmed again and the sadist was redeployed away from any other possible encounters with these lovely and innocent animals.

My father had a special reason to be thankful to his pony. As he continued with the tale of his equine workmate, Dad told me he was driving some materials in a roadway which led to the coalface one morning, Dick suddenly stopped abruptly and refused to move another inch forward. Just a minute or two later, a huge and lethal shard of rock crashed through the roof of the roadway. Known colloquially by generations of coal miners as 'pot-holes', these pieces of rock could be six to ten metres long and just as wide. They fell frequently and without warning, killing many men. One particular Yorkshire pit pony had other ideas that morning, leading my dad's new found appreciation of 'horse sense'.

A man called Frank Linfoot trained Dad to become a

rope splicer and Dad started his apprenticeship in the field of mines mechanics in 1945, just as he joined his first working men's club. Part of the tragedy for the generation of coal miners who followed was that, when Margaret Thatcher achieved her aim in closing down the mines – and all the country's other heavy industry for that matter – the skills the miners had learned were of little or no use elsewhere and years of unemployment and waste was the result. A rope splicer's duties involved looking after thousands of yards of metal rope, as well as installing endless rope haulage systems, driven by bulky and powerful engines. The rope haulages featured monorail systems and 'coolicars'. Most commonly those of us who used the endless rope haulage systems, as I myself did early on during my time down the pit, made use of huge metal clips. An integral part of my duties as a 'timber-lad' was to be able to fasten the clip to the rope and I would attach the other end to whatever was being transported.

When extending the rope (which was referred to as 'moving up') or shortening the rope, an item called a 'sylvester' was used. This was a device around three feet long which would stretch the rope and hold it in place. It was applied with the aid of a cranking handle. The sword part of the device was equipped with huge and sharp metal teeth. When the sylvester was released after use, the sword would fly through the air at great speed. That was the time to get out of the way, unless you knew what you were doing. My first wife's uncle was hit in the chest with a flying sylvester sword and he spent a long time in hospital fighting for his life. Accidents with sylvesters were all too common, mainly either due to bad maintenance practices or lack of skill.

In all his time down the pit, Dad was never hit by a sylvester sword. The only accidents he suffered consisted of getting fragments of rope in his eyes and on another occasion, whilst moving a spool of rope, the whole gubbins rolled onto his hand, fracturing many bones and slicing off a finger. Once back on the surface in the medical room, the ambulance man Raymond Greatorex asked me to locate Dad's missing finger. Predictably the digit was still in his safety glove and I emptied it out into the palm of my hand and popped it into an ice-bag, which went off to hospital with Dad in the hope that it could have been re-attached. Unfortunately for Dad, this was not possible.

As a young man, Dad was taught to remain in charge of his faculties while alcohol was being served. His own father, my grandfather, was a solid Christian and regularly quoted the bible and Saint Paul, and who was fond of saying, "Drink a Little Wine for Thy Stomach's Sake." My grandad always imbibed, but preached caution in terms of all things alcoholic. Another of his cautionary sayings was when he used to advise his son, "Get the better of the beer, don't let the beer get the better of you." I have subsequently passed these words of wisdom down to my own son Steven, although in all honesty I haven't always followed Grandad's advice too closely myself.

Meanwhile back down Nostell Colliery, I was told

about my great-grandfather Joe White, who was my grandmother's father. Just as I heard a million more reminiscences which always followed when my dad had the time and the inclination, the sandwiches and the coffee from our flasks was finished and it was time to walk through some air doors, back into the tunnel where the overtime job on something called an endless rope haulage system needing to be completed.

I never heard anyone speak an ill word about Dad, until long after his death, when the bellicose ramblings of an angry drunk man in a pub in the village of Crofton near Wakefield was both bewildering and deeply upsetting. Showing off to his pals, there were loads of barbed insults about me, which is water off a duck's back to be honest. I couldn't remember for the life of me who this idiot was, but there is at least one in every village and he was clearly Crofton's own representative in the field of community idiocy.

This odd-looking chap started spouting his bile and vitriol over what was probably his tenth pint. Drinking on an empty head is never a good idea. The subject was utter garbage and ridiculous lies about my late father. In my younger and more fiery days, this loud and lairy individual wouldn't have rambled his way through the first sentence of his nonsense before I would have dragged him outside and showed him the extent of both my pugilistic ability and my truly horrid temper.

On that occasion there were two factors saving this moron from a severe beating:

A. The pub had CCTV cameras up everywhere and I

wouldn't have risked my collar felt in order to simply beat up such a cheap and totally irrelevant figure, despite all his loud bluster and verbal diarrhoea.

B. I was being treated for PTSD at the local psychiatric hospital at the time and an arrest for violent crime may well have been linked to my illness. I was in such a mess at that time that I may even have ended up being sectioned under the Mental Health Act. As I look back on that incident now, I realise I had very little control over myself and my emotions. The medication helped, but was also stymied and somewhat negated by the level of alcohol I was consuming at the time.

After all is said and done, this idiot was telling ridiculous stories and bullshit lies about my own father, a highly respected man. But with a wife to protect and a reputation with a stain or two on it already, I did the right thing in walking quietly away, deciding on this very rare occasion in my life that discretion was indeed the better part of valour.

*

# 3

# A bedrock
# of talent

Dad told me many stories of the early Clubland artistes in post-war Britain and about the time that rock'n'roll was born, when variety entertainers began to look towards the clubs for their earning opportunities as the pre-war circuit of variety theatres fell like a stack of dominos. Something huge was developing and the stories from both my parents, as well as those of my uncle and my beloved grandad whetted my appetite. I couldn't wait to reach the age of 18 and the rites of passage moment when I could join my father for a pint at the local club.

On the maternal side of my family, the links with Clubland were even stronger. My grandad Edward Margrave was known as 'Whistling Ted Marlowe' and the reputation of his fine tenor voice and well-crafted songs went before him. But as the late 1950s heralded the arrival of the new rock'n'roll and skiffle boom in popular music, Whistling Ted was typical of so many people who had worked their way up in the variety theatre, only to find that most people wanted to hear the new groups and singers and not old-style variety entertainers.

My grandad had been part of a tenor/baritone duet along with a man called Maurice Riding. Mr Riding's career was ended when his wife flew into a jealous rage at some indiscretion or other and promptly ripped up all his musical arrangements. Whistling Ted went solo, but by then with his best days onstage behind him, my grandad also took over stewardship of a club in Wakefield. The singing engagements were restricted to local clubs only, to which he either travelled to and from by train or occasionally pedalling his pushbike, complete with his musical arrangements in the saddle bag and his suit thrown over his shoulder inside a suitable waterproof cover.

One of my earliest childhood memories of my grandfather was of him playing gramophone records in the flat he shared with my grandma. His favourite 'modern singer' was Jim Reeves and he didn't get into rock'n'roll bands, choosing instead to declare The Bachelors as his favourite group. As I revealed in my autobiography, years later I was to work on theatre tours with The Bachelors. Grandad would have been as proud as punch!

My grandma had always been a hard-working mill lady. She baked delicious meals, with her meat and potato pie being a real favourite of mine. Grandma collapsed to her death one afternoon during a heatwave in the late summer of 1976 as she had just left the local hairdresser's. Grandma suffered from angina and her kind heart just stopped.

Grandad didn't talk much about his days in showbusiness or the horrors he experienced in the trenches during the First World War. My boyhood days spent in his company were made up of us playing cricket on his garden path, where we used his front gate as the wickets. Grandad always used to fascinate me with tricks he had somehow convinced his budgie Joey to perform. Sadly, Grandad died in 1979 and I miss him still.

He was one of many hundreds of variety artistes who were unseated by variety producers and promoters during the late 1950s onwards. So many of them wanted to feed the hunger for rock'n'roll. Many of them discovered that the mainly younger music fans did not want to sit through variety acts and musical speciality acts, magicians and other assorted 'variety turns' in order to wait for their favourite rock'n'roll stars to finally hit the stage. The smarter promoters knew instead that hiring concert halls and dance halls would ensure that a young and hip crowd could gather for non-stop music to dance to.

*

# 4

# Picking up the pace of growth

As the 1960s began more and more clubs were working on the concert room section of their businesses by hiring resident musicians to play for dance nights and to accompany visiting cabaret artistes.

The first club I joined was Ryhill and Havercroft social club, which was always known locally as 'The Legion'. The facilities included a car park and a small foyer which led to a large concert room. In adjacent rooms there was a games room, equipped with a snooker table. There was a lounge area, which was always known as the 'best room', and one or two other nooks and crannies.

Such clubs were run by a club steward and vacancies for club's stewards and married couples were favoured in the role. I'm not sure how lawful the criteria involved in whether or not people could be hired was. It is with great certainly the club committee men, who made the decision on which people to employ was worded very clearly in order to indicate who was supposedly in charge.

*So and So working men's club requires a
Steward and wife to assist. Accommodation
provided as part of the job. Wages negotiable.*

Some of the appointments wreaked of nepotism. Some
club officials knew very well that by planting a family
member on the inside of the money and the decisions
often meant that personal money became conveniently
mixed up with that which by rights belonged to the club.

Aside from the gentlemen of the committee, clubs
were obligated to include pillars of society when it came
to looking after the finances of the individual club. These
men were known as trustees and I'm pretty sure that
many of them would indeed be trustworthy. There were
exceptions in the club which I become of a member of
the committee for, which really should have been
foreseen, such as the appointment of a man called Alec.
This was really a huge error all round. Alec's dad was a
hard-working pit-man and he did his utmost to help gain
scholarships for his two sons, Alec and Peter. Peter did
well in life but Alec did not. Alec was a botanist who
wrote many books and lectured on the subject but he was
also a drunk. His was a wasted life and Alec spent much
of it on the dole.

Some people might say that electing an out of work
alcoholic onto the committee of a working men's club was
in point of fact, a contradiction of terms. The temptation
to misappropriate club funds would have been strong and
hard to resist.

I should say I was always friendly with Alec and he to

me. I bore him no malice, but such was Alec's love affair with booze and his apparently unwillingness to make his mark, as men of his education are surely capable of, that this made him a financial liability who was anything but the trustworthy trustee he tried to present himself as. Alec held court in a small lounge bar at the club on Station Road in Ryhill. Those around him included John Osbourne and Reggie Mallinder, two likely lads who just laughed along at Alec's towering intellect. It always seemed to be that John and Reggie were both selected to be in Alec's inner-circle of drinking buddies, due to the fact they were intellectually no match for him.

Alec liked to provide the conversational direction with only occasional contributions from others being tolerated. Alec told the story that he had invited some Jehovah's Witnesses into his home on Westfields in Ryhill one morning. He made then tea and then told them all the doors were locked and that he was effectively keeping them hostage. Alec then informed them of his views on what he described as the holes in the theories of the movement and the alleged sexual shenanigans of those involved.

One of those held under temporary house arrest by Mr Wall was Peter Knowles. Peter had been a top professional footballer tipped for stardom and England caps. Peter came from a nearby village, which was called Fitzwilliam and which was the home of one of the nation's richest social clubs of the 1970s, Hemsworth miners welfare club, known locally as 'The Pit Club'. Alec only released his hostages once he had given them all a piece of his mind. That was just the type of person he was.

Peter Knowles played football in the top flight for Wolverhampton Wanderers and his brother Cyril played for Tottenham Hotspur. Cyril was the subject of the terrace song which became a hit record 'Nice One Cyril'. Peter packed in playing football as soon as he became a Jehovah's Witness. Perhaps Alec Wall may have thought he could persuade Peter Knowles to slam on the brakes in his religious activities and get back out on the football pitch, but alas it never happened and football lost a major star. The Jehovah's Witnesses gained a major bargaining chip, with so many people who knew Knowles apparently thinking that, if it was good enough for this extremely skilful and clean-cut football star, life in the Jehovah's Witnesses may just prove good enough for them.

Family parties, senior citizens functions, seaside club trips, sports teams and a panoply of other events had all sprung up in the working men's clubs. As small children we first became aware of local clubs by virtue of the children's Christmas party, where there was always a present from Santa and a visit from a conjuror or children's entertainer of some sort.

The club trip was the highlight of the summer, as we all boarded a fleet of hired coaches and headed for the seaside. My dad was a member of all three clubs in our village and around 30 to 40 coaches parked at the side of the main road outside the club, just waiting for parents and kids to clamber onboard and head to Scarborough, Blackpool, Bridlington or Cleethorpes. The numbered coaches were all complete with crates of pop and packets of crisps for all the kids and off we went in convoy, heading for the coast.

One particular trip is stuck in my mind for all the right reasons. We headed for Scarborough and my sister, six years older than me, was already out doing her Saturday job at Gebhards butchers on Wakefield market. My mum was working close by in a shoe shop close to the indoor market hall. That just left my dad and I to join the trip and head off to the Yorkshire coast. The problem was there was a strike going on in the pits then and money was tight. My father and I spent a great day together, strolling around Peasholm park and on the beach, but mainly walking here there and everywhere. A weather alert was promising huge electric thunderstorms all around us on that hot summer afternoon, and as the clouds began to look threatening, Dad decreed that a walk up many steps towards St Mary's church, which stands close to Scarborough castle, was a good idea.

Scarborough began its tourist life as a spa town and people used to go there for the fresh air and a purgative in the spa water, which was said to be an effective treatment for everything from tuberculosis to athlete's foot. A literary figure interred in the graveyard at St Mary's visited for such a cure but had not survived the experience and died in Scarborough. Anne Brontë, who penned *The Tenant of Wildfell Hall*, was the youngest of the famous Brontë sisters from Haworth in West Yorkshire. Her grave is sought out by visitors from all the world as the literary-minded make their pilgrimage to

Scarborough in their thousands, although thankfully not all at once, and are seen tramping around the graveyard at St Mary's in search of her final resting place.

The story goes that Miss Brontë went on holiday in Scarborough for a long break, which was intended to alleviate what was then called pthisis or consumption and is now more commonly known as tuberculosis. Brontë died in a Scarborough lodging house known as Wood's in 1849. The site where the building once stood is now completely covered by the huge landmark that is the Grand Hotel. Queen Victoria once stayed there when this huge establishment was first built and where, rather less notably, I used to perform regularly in cabaret in their lovely ballroom, which also boasts theatre style seating upstairs and which provides a superb vantage point for those who wish to 'people watch' rather than dance.

Upwards Dad and I strode on that golden day of the club trip to Scarborough, ascending the many steps to St Mary's Church, after starting out at the harbourside and making our way up the cobbled byway of Princess Street, we headed ever onwards and upwards. Good strong shoes were essential and on that particular day, I was wearing a lovely strong pair of brand-new footwear, complete with fancy red laces.

A day or two before the club trip my dad had to scratch around a bit to find enough money to kit me out in the new shoes. Being on strike we were still luckier than most, with my mother working, and Dad and I had boarded the Yorkshire traction bus, making the short journey to the nearby village of Royston near Barnsley, where we had been told about a shop doing a special offer on boys and girl's shoes while the strike was still on. The shoes were very plain, but made of good leather and the man in the shop, as if to leaven the plain look of the shoes, had taken out the boring black laces and replaced them with bright red ones.

On the day of the club trip, sporting my fancy red laces we arrived at St Mary's just in time. The storm had hit and there were lightning strikes all over the east coast that summer afternoon. While others sought shelter by crowding into amusement arcades, my wise and knowledgeable father had the nous and the presence of mind to realise that St Mary's church was one of the few buildings on Scarborough's south bay which was kitted out with a lightning conductor. As ever the church was open to visitors and we took shelter, along with a selection of other weather-savvy day trippers. The storm subsided just in time for us to head to the coach park and join our fellow club trippers for the journey home.

That same summer on the following week it was the turn of the Liberal club just up the road in our village to head for their annual trip to the seaside. The destination that year was Blackpool and, to the shock of people arriving at the roadside to board the transportation, awaiting them were not the usual nice coaches supplied by local firm WR&P Bingley. Instead we were all asked instead to clamber on board Yorkshire traction service buses, which were not all that comfortable for the bum-numbing two hour-plus journey to the Fylde coast. Known locally as 'pit paddies', these buses were used as transportation for mining contractors and others travelling from pit to pit. Many of the bus seats were coated in grime and pit-muck and had clearly not been cleaned. The ladies resplendent in their summer dresses were unimpressed to say the very least.

Off we all went, but I was told later that the club secretary, a rather severe man called Dick Vincent who I knew because he was caretaker at my school, had a flea in his ear once everyone returned that evening with their summer-wear Sunday best togs coated in grime.

The seaside resorts were packed with trippers and holiday-makers throughout what was known as the Wakes Weeks, when the factories and mills took their holidays. Side by side on the beach with workmates, neighbours and friends was simply how things were done then.

All the clubs within the heavy industrial areas sponsored or assisted such family leisure activities by providing funds and facilities for local community clubs. There were dockers' clubs in the ports, steel-workers' clubs around the North East of England, South Wales and of course in South Yorkshire, where steel had been synonymous with the city of Sheffield seemingly forever.

The various steelworks covered a huge area of the Tinsley, Darnall and Wincobank areas of the city. Today the vast majority of the steel industry has been uprooted, mothballed or the trade taken by German and French steelworks, who all seemed very keen to make all the steel, continue to mine the coal, tell the British we had to shut our industries down so we could become a service economy. Call centres and giant Meadowhall shopping centre now cover the ground where much of the old steelworks once stood. Bits of the once proud industry were sold off to venture capitalists, who stripped it all down and cherry-picked all the best bits.

After all that, who needed the steel-workers' clubs like Sheffield Foundry workers club, Bright Steels club and all the rest? As a result, dozens more club and entertainment venues toppled like dominos and are now gone forever. So many community assets have been lost forever.

\*

# 5

# So who wants to run the place?

By 1972 the C&IU discovered they had around 4,500 clubs operating independently but under their protective umbrella in the UK. Men were coming forward in droves to become involved in the running of the local clubs. The problem was of course that so many lacked any degree of competence, knowledge, business acumen and perhaps most crucially, honesty.

Many clubs became a target for those willing to get stuck into the tills. There was gaming machine money to count, banking to be done and a million other fiddles on gambling games, bingo, draw or tote tickets and the like. This was crime and this was embezzlement on a grand scale. Many got caught with their hands on the till, while others managed to remain undiscovered for donkey's years. Visiting comedians could often be heard to quip onstage that the first prize in the raffle was "a week serving on the committee".

At one time or another my own personal involvement

in Clubland was as a committee member and concert secretary of a working men's club. I was also a non-league football player for a WMC side and then a miners' welfare team. I was a keen member of a miners' welfare crown green bowling team and I held membership of several WMCs at one and the same time.

I have almost always held a C&IU pass card, renewed annually, which guarantees the bearer visitation rights and limited associate membership privileges within any club the bearer may wish to visit in the entire UK. All provided the club chosen for a visit was under the umbrella of the C&IU of course.

At one and the same period I was performing in a Clubland covers band while doing some representation work for agents, which involved selling acts to clubs and being paid on a commission basis for every act I sold. I was also booking the acts for Ryhill WMC and the club had begun to do well again, after quite a lull in its fortunes. The business weathercock seemed set fair at Ryhill WMC until we (the committee) made the collective mistake of hiring a new club steward. His name was Bunny and his 'wife to assist' was a vivacious blonde lady called June. Under their stewardship the club seemed busier, but the takings were not rising accordingly.

We laid a trap for Bunny and he walked straight into it. A few days before a beer delivery was due, we brought in a weights and measures man to sample the quality and strength of the ales. It seemed that through an elaborate gas and piping system, Bunny had been watering everything down – indeed, for weeks customers had been complaining about the quality of the draught beers. A stock check was also way out, and Bunny and June were soon booted out, ready to inflict their dishonest bag of business tricks on someone else.

If a club steward and a club treasurer or secretary were in cahoots, the result for the club could be devastating. This was the case in countless clubs, which seemed to fold whilst still doing well in terms of bums on seats.

The only time when there was any hope of making changes in the hierarchy was when it was time for the election of officials and committee members. In many communities there was a cachet in wearing the badge of office. Some clubs even had club blazers and ties made for their 'committee men'. It was always men who were elected. Women were not allowed to stand for the committee and this is still the case in many clubs even today in what we believe to be more enlightened times.

The truth is that many of the remaining clubs do not even elect officials anymore. Apathy reigns and people just don't want to be involved anymore, so when folk actually do come forward to offer help in running a club, they are most usually co-opted onto the management committee and at so many of the surviving clubs, there are always vacancies in the committee rooms.

*

# 6

# The blue touchpaper
# is lit

During the massive growth period of the clubs the C&IU magazine *Club Journal* ran many articles on the transition between smaller premises to the pleasure palaces being built in the new Clubland. The journal's writers examined the development of club premises and there were many reports of wooden huts and tin-roofed buildings being swept away and replaced by luxury facilities as opulent as any which could be found anywhere in the world at that time.

Reports in the magazine during the sixties singled out clubs such as The Brun Grove club in Blackpool for particular praise, and by the time I came into Clubland, most of the tin-huts and wooden shack clubs had already been knocked down and replaced with the more swish and modern premises. Some of them retained the memories of their humble roots by hanging on to their original names. For instance, Mapplewell and district ex-servicemen's club near Barnsley started life as 'The Tin

Hat' club. This was a nod towards the work of ARP air-raid wardens, who used to wander around communities at night looking for exposed lights, during the time Hitler's Luftwaffe was bombing the crap out of us. Those familiar with the classic sit-com *Dad's Army* will know about the power-crazed greengrocer Mr Hodges who paraded around bedecked by his tin hat in Walmington-on-Sea.

Across working-class Britain in the 1960s the clubs were attracting new members from a generation of baby boomers, with so many families looking to establish a social life which matched their other aspirations.

With breweries virtually throwing money at the clubs in the form of low interest loans and preferential barrelage discounts, the clubs had many people queuing at the doors on concert nights. 'House full' signs were common for shows featuring some of the biggest of the club stars. I go into great detail and name just a few of the club-filling performers and acts much further on in this story.

The concert chairman, so parodied by comedian Colin Crompton in the Granada TV show hit, *The Wheel-tappers and Shunters Social Club*, ruled the roost. Often armed with a bell, these men would sit in their box, controlling curtains and lights and introducing the acts. Hardly any had showbusiness experience and some of their introductions left much to be desired.

The club announcements were called out over the microphone in the chairman's box, with instructions such as "No standing near the bar!" and "Bingo cards are now on sale!" The exhortation was often announced during the performance of whoever was onstage at the time. This meant that all of a sudden, we entertainers found ourselves trying to entertain a moving target, with people starting to mill around the room. Sometimes bingo cards were sold at the front of the stage while the artistes were performing. This meant that us 'turns' found ourselves trying to engage with and entertain a large gossiping queue of folk.

Some concert chairmen gave a warning or two to any audience that he adjudged was being too noisy whilst the artiste was onstage. Some chairmen were even known to stop the performer onstage in full flow, so he could demand loudly that everyone present should "Give Order!"

Making any noise whatsoever while the bingo was on created consternation from dabber-wielding devotees. I even heard one chairman announce loudly, "If you want to talk while the bingo is on either go in the other room or wait till the 'turn' comes back on!"

Some clubs presenting live entertainment were armed with the best of intentions. Moorends comrades club in Cleckheaton near Bradford had an illuminated sign outside their concert room door, bearing the slogan 'PLEASE DO NOT ENTER WHEN THE ARTISTE IS ONSTAGE'. Many years after my first visit to this club I spent my saddest New Year's Eve ever. I was booked there on good money, only to find a sad and tiny trickle of people had bothered to turn up to make up the entire audience. When midnight arrived, 'Auld Lang Sang' was sung by about a dozen or so patrons.

The concert chairmen were often unintentionally comical. One night I was a member of the audience at a club in the Yorkshire village of South Hiendley, where I had made the short journey from my own home village to see an act called The Two Good Reasons. The act consisted of two singing guitarists who were really rather good. The chairman made his monotone announcement to begin the show, "For your entertainment tonight – The Reasons." The two men onstage looked at each other and in quite a loud voice one of them said, "That's not our name." The chairman looked puzzled and then a light seemed to dawn in his eyes. "Sorry ladies and gentlemen, I meant to say, for your entertainment tonight, The Two Reasons." The lads onstage rolled their eyes and shouted across at the chairman, "That's still not our name!" The chairman then looked somewhat perplexed, before the lads gave him another clue by asking, "Are we 'bad' or 'good'?" Over the microphone and offending many of those who were shocked by the language, the poor chairman replied in exasperation, "How do I know, I haven't fuckin' seen you yet!"

On another confidence sapping evening in Barnsley, I was standing on stage behind the curtains at one club venue, waiting to be introduced by the concert chairman when I heard the chairman make this announcement over the club PA system: "Good evening and welcome to our Sunday evening concert. Before we bring the artiste onstage, I would just like to announce that the committee have now done something about the terrible turns we have been getting lately. From next weekend we have a new agent supplying us with turns. Tonight's turn is the last from the old agent . . . best of order please for Mark Ritchie!"

One night at St Patricks club in the Yorkshire town of Hemsworth, I was introduced onstage by a chairman who announced, "He is back by request. I don't think he's much cop but some of you might like him, best of order please for Mark Ritchie!" It was a prosperous club which seemed to go downhill fast, suggesting some form of major dishonesty in regard to the integrity or otherwise from some of the gentlemen of the committee. The land the club once occupied is now covered by a frozen food outlet.

In many of the Catholic social clubs, the concert chairman weren't always completely in charge. I remember a visit to The Holy Name social club in Hull. I was booked to perform a comedy spot in the middle of an evening of entertainment, which was being topped and tailed by a pop group consisting of four young lads. The priest stood near the bar armed with a large glass of whisky, which seemed to be topped up at very regular intervals. The band played their opening song and the two lads on guitars at the front were also the singers. One lad shouted his greetings to the packed auditorium by announcing, "Hi everyone – I'm Andy Norfolk!" His bandmate then came in with, "And I'm Dave Good and together we are Norfolk 'n' Good!"

The priest stiffened and blanched at what is in fact one of the oldest gags on the world. Weaving and staggering towards the stage, the good father was waving his arms and announcing loudly: "That's it, lads. You are off. I told you no dirty language is allowed in this club." The lads looked confused and disconsolate and, grumbling all the way, broke their gear down and packed it quickly into their van, before driving off with the angry priest's words still ringing in their ears.

I myself had a warning before going onstage one night at the Corpus Christi club in Leeds. The good father there warned me in no uncertain terms to "keep it clean or go home!"

So many priests seem perfectly able to control what people say and do, even after consuming copious amounts of alcohol. The only warning I ever received in a Catholic club from a sober priest was in the lovely Maltby Catholic club near Rotherham. The priest had just arrived from his native Zimbabwe and the evening of my visit was only his second time in attendance at the club. This priest gave me a pep-talk before the show, which consisted of informing me that the entertainer who had been onstage the week before had used "gross profanities". I was on my best behaviour that night, with no such profanity indiscretions from me, and the evening passed off surprisingly well as I walked on comedy eggshells.

The Arundel ex-servicemen's club in Sheffield is still open today and boasts a very large concert room. A lovely man called Roy, who everyone nicknamed 'Pugwash', was always in the box and made the job of entertaining this large and notoriously unresponsive audience much easier than it could have been for the visiting acts. When Roy died, a new bloke took over the concert chairmen duties. An assortment of data processor-type signs advertised the upcoming shows as well as declaring the name of whoever was onstage on any particular evening. On my last ever visit to the club, the new guy in the chairman's box made an announcement which went as follows: "Good evening ladies and gentlemen, and tonight we have our Thursday night spectacular show. To start the show tonight we have someone who is no stranger to this club. He's been before many times and I don't see what's spectacular about him, but here he is anyway, Mark Ritchie!"

Another evening in Wigan, Lancashire, was also memorable for all the wrong reasons. Waiting to go on, I heard the chairman announce, "Ladies and gentlemen, welcome to Sunday night at the club. I know this is a very difficult evening for all of us. As many of you already know, our popular club treasurer Ronnie dropped dead in the club this afternoon while selling the raffle tickets. His wife Lily is sitting with us tonight as usual, as she is sure Ronnie would not want her to miss her Sunday night at the club and her games of bingo. I am now going to ask for everyone to stand as our resident musicians Sid on organ and Pete on drums play 'Abide with Me', after which I will be asking for a minute's silence to be observed."

'Abide with Me' was played, the sobs were audible and the minute's silence was observed impeccably. Next came the scraping of chairs as everyone sat down and the chairman announced, "And now live onstage, here is a funny man from Yorkshire who is going to make you laugh. We are in for a good night tonight folks, so please welcome Mark Ritchie!"

I walked out to the sound of snuffling, sniffing and sobbing and the sight of a line of well-wishers, all queuing to hug the aforementioned Lily, who was seated right at the front of the stage. The tearful tissue action lasted for ages. At the end of the evening Lily was getting another port and lemon from the bar as I walked out towards my car. She stopped me in my tracks, hugged me warmly and thanked me for "giving Ronnie a great send-off".

Different areas all had clubs that catered for regional workforces. The venue names were accurate yet sometimes comical. Over the years I worked at The Carriage and Waggon welfare club in Derby, the Excelsior Crisps club in Grimsby, the Hartlepool boilermakers club, the Sheffield foundry workers club, the Pop and Pastie social club in Keighley and the Rotherham borough transport club to name but a few. The list was endless, the memories of these long-lost pleasure palaces remain intact.

Sometimes during a concert night, if a visiting entertainer was positioned in the appropriate spot, they could learn much about what the audience thought of them. One evening at Bradford City brass band club, I had just completed the first half of the show. With no toilet facilities backstage, I found myself installed within the narrow confines of a cubicle in the concert room toilet. Occupying the perfect spot for eavesdropping, I heard the urinators coming and going from the trough.

One man standing at the trough greeted a friend who had missed the first half and was spending a penny prior to a mid-evening bingo session getting going. The conversation began with the usual matey chat, before the newly arrived bloke asked, "What's t'turn like?" I pricked up my ears and awaited the reply, which came after quite a pause for thought, with both urinators completely unaware of my presence behind the closed cubicle door. This is what I heard: "He's been here before. He's alright . . . if you like laughing."

Not only was talent a prerequisite when working the clubs, skin as thick as a rhinoceros also came in handy too sometimes. Only the strong or the stupid survived. As one wise man once wrote, stupidity has saved many a man from insanity.

I have met some talented yet very stupid entertainers in my time. Who knows, perhaps some people may consider me one of them. Certainly to survive on the working men's club scene for any length of time, you need a motive for being there. Mine was always the money. I treat entertaining folk as a job. Some do it for the ego trip, others do it as a bit of a sideline. Many don't last long, while others survive, enjoy career longevity and at the end they emerge largely unscathed from what can be a pretty humbling series of humiliating experiences.

I have sometimes been accused of being too hard and cynical, while those who know me well with attest to me being comparable to crème brulée, in that although I might appear rock hard whilst onstage and doing my thing, once off stage I have a surprisingly soft centre.

Those who take themselves too seriously in Clubland are doomed. I never have. I have survived and many of my experiences have actually shaped who I am. As a performer you can go onstage and become someone else for a while. For some of us, that is a useful thing to do. Self-knowledge is everything and I like myself more than I used to when I was young and harder to know.

Working men's club stages provide a place in which to perform, for anyone who has a dream. The fact is that aside from Jane McDonald, who I shall come to later, no one has made their way out of the clubs and on to the telly for years. As the clubs fade further into obscurity, the dreams of so many have become lost in the ether of show business past.

*

# 7

# Are you
# a member?

Working men's clubs operate as private members clubs, meaning they must keep and maintain a record of their visitors. The great Clubland institution of employing a doorman is a legal requirement, although more honoured in the breach than in the observance, a line written by Shakespeare for Hamlet, Prince of Denmark to speak, whilst opining in the play that some rules really should be enforced more rigorously than others.

The job of doorman in many hundreds of clubs was often given to retired people who wanted to earn a few quid in order to top up their woefully inadequate pensions. Nowadays technology has done its thing, as automatic keyfob door releases are frequently used to ensure that visitors have to ring the doorbell. This will prompt someone in authority to go to the door and decide whether or not to grant admittance.

I remember a heck of a hullaballoo only a few years

ago at the East Ward labour club in Bradford, when I turned up to perform at a Sunday lunchtime gig. The club stands at the side of a busy road not all that far from the city centre. The normal routine for visiting entertainers was to drive around the back, where a door next to a smoking shelter would be opened and we acts would then have the task of lugging our PA systems and other equipment in, all the way through the length of the concert room, down to the well-appointed and roomy stage.

On this my umpteenth visit to this Bradford club, things were a little different to the norm. There seemed to be a large crowd gathering around the main entrance. I wondered if local public transport had just dropped off a bus-load of punters, as I knew it was Ramadan at the time and that the mainly Muslim taxi drivers of Bradford were not all that keen on working too many hours. I drove around the back and I thought I had driven into World War 3, with gangs of men and women trying and failing to gain admittance to the rear entrance of the club

I have known Travellers and Gypsies all my life and went to school with a few, and I know that there are those who give a bad name that the others unfortunately have to suffer. It transpired that the ruckus in Bradford was just such an example where a piece of land belonging to the club had been camped on by Travellers. The field at the rear of the club then led down to a small wall where the Travellers had decided to use the gap between the garden wall and the club premises wall as an open toilet. The scrum at the front door turned out to be more of the

Travellers trying to get in through the main entrance, only to be met by a brave yet elderly doorman, who informed them that WMCs were and always had been members only and resolutely refused to release the automatic door.

The problem was that legitimate members couldn't get in either and the police were soon called. I managed to gain admittance through a side door and the show eventually went ahead. On a future visit to the club a few months later, I chatted to the doorman about the whole catalogue of events which took place during my last visit. The club had to shell out lots of cash on metal lockable gates to prevent any future unwanted visits on the land. Protective suits, clothing and chemicals were then bought to clean up the excrement and the rubbish which the clandestine visitors had left behind. The bill, which I saw, was ferocious. On the day the metal gates arrived, I heard later, on realising they were soon to be marooned on the strip of land they had moved onto and unable to go in or out of it, the members of the travelling fraternity soon made their exit.

There were clubs that admitted Travellers and Gypsies as club members, but it was a decision that was not always well received. Many years ago, Westerton Road WMC near Leeds did this but most of the other club members, objecting to their presence, kept out of the place in protest and the club closed its doors permanently only months later.

Park and Arbourthorne club in Sheffield used to stand on a very short strip of City Road between The Manor social club on one side and the Arundel ex-servicemen's club on the other. Up until around 20 years ago all three clubs were run successfully, with all three booking the top acts and bands on the circuit. The area around the clubs is dominated by the sprawling Manor housing estate, and back then the place had acquired a reputation for trouble and crime. Very wisely the committees of all three clubs operated a policy that anyone barred from one club would be barred from them all. Things were going swimmingly, until Park and Arbourthorne club changed tack and started allowing certain local ne'er-do-wells in. The club went to wrack and ruin in no time and closed soon after.

No car or van in living memory has lasted more than half an hour on the car park at the rear of The Manor social club in Sheffield. With a tramline at the front of the club, parking on the road is not an option. The doorman occupies a tiny hutch in the corner next to the front door and visiting artistes are advised to park on the pavement right next to the front door, with the bonnet of their vehicle under the doorman's nose and with cameras recording who comes and goes. Whenever I have visited this particular venue, I always buy the doorman a pint, which I like to think assures me of his best endeavours in terms of dissuading the local cavemen in the area from damaging or stealing my vehicle.

My final tale of the humble Clubland doormen goes to Nostell miners' welfare club near Wakefield where, for a short time, a man I knew personally acted as doorman in the evenings. During the day Denis Brook could usually be found underground at Nostell colliery, where my dad also worked and, for my sins and for a while at least, so did I. In the same way that the legendary Polish-born Hollywood film producer Samuel Goldwyn used to mangle the English language with his misunderstood and mispronounced declarations, so did Denis. Goldwyn came from Eastern European stock and his grasp of the English language could be somewhat patchy, producing utterances which became known as 'Goldwynisms'. Examples of which included him informing a legal representative that "a verbal contract wasn't worth the paper it was written on". He also told someone making a western that "you can always get more Indians from the reservoir".

Denis was Yorkshire through and through. Always smart and dapper, he was a bachelor and he lived with his mum. It wasn't that Denis mispronounced words and phrases, it was more that he didn't think through how to articulate what he actually wanted to say. Sitting in the doorman's box one evening at the club, Denis greeted a visitor he did not recognise by enquiring casually if he was a member. The man replied that he was not and could he please sign in. Denis immediately produced a visitors' book and began to feel around in his pockets for a pen. Realising he had forgotten his own, Denis asked the visitor if he had a pen on him. It was now the visitors turn to feel around in his pockets, but alas he did not have a pen either. Denis replied in true 'Denis the Doorman' style by instructing the man with these words, "Oh never mind, you can sign in when you leave."

As I wrote in my autobiography *Right Place...Wrong Time*, Denis was killed in an underground accident at Nostell colliery in 1981. I was working in the safety department at the time and the piece of rolling stock machinery which hit Denis at speed, crushing the life out of him, was towed up a drift (a long sharp hill) to the surface for inspection. After the piece of equipment was examined, it was I who drew the short straw and had to wash Denis's blood off the metal frame of the equipment that claimed his life. I liked Denis. I think we were kindred spirits as neither of us liked being down the pit very much.

Nowadays the doormen aren't anywhere near as fiercely efficient as they once were. The rites of passage within the working-class communities of old determined that almost invariably sons followed dads and grandads into club membership when they reached 18. Nowadays no one can drag most average older teenagers into the clubs. I regularly find myself thinking regretfully but unsurprisingly that my own son never followed me into club membership and that he now has a son of his own. I think perhaps by the time my grandson Mathew reaches his majority, there may be not a single working men's club to join even if he wanted to.

*

# 8

# The mystery and
# the glamour

J ust as theatre variety, summer season end-of-the-pier
shows and the like provided a special atmosphere for
those of us old enough to recall, a concert night in a
WMC during its heydays also took some beating.

In the 1960s/70s those of us lucky enough to go off on
family holidays often got to see a show or two. My family
once tried a holiday at Butlin's camp, which was situated
just outside the genteel resort of Filey on the Yorkshire
coast. A curious rock formation snakes out into the sea
in Filey, creating tidal protection for fun and games for
all the family on what is surely one of the best sandy
beaches in the whole of England. Butlin's didn't work out
well for us, as we were all stricken with food poisoning
and our tiny chalet soon became 'Projectile Vomit City
Central' – until we packed our bags and abandoned our
holiday by heading back home on the train, throwing up
all along the way.

The summer shows which my family saw in

Scarborough, Blackpool, Torquay, Bridlington and Great Yarmouth featured long forgotten stars such as Donald Peers, Jimmy Clitheroe, Two-Ton Tessie O'Shea, Val Doonican, Tommy Steele, Billy Dainty, Ken Platt and many others.

We had to purchase tickets for the theatre shows of course and when people pay to see something, they almost invariably want to enjoy themselves. Going to see a show in WMC was very different. No one paid to go in most of them, with the cost of live entertainment and music staged 52 weeks a year being factored into the disproportionately low annual membership charges. The feeling of entitlement from the Clubland people made me realise the rationale of club folk, who exclaimed indignantly, "We are not paying to go into our own clubs!"

On the telly back then were prime-time shows that reflected the nation's live light entertainment. *The Black and White Minstrel Show*, which was a homage to the minstrels shows of 1920s American vaudeville. Such shows do not exist anymore, frowned upon today for very good reason due to the black-faced minstrels, who were white men who had blacked up with make-up, and the stereotyping of seeing those with black faces singing musical numbers in which they kissed and chased the white girl singers/dancers.

Producer Barney Colehan presented a show on BBC called *The Good Old Days*, in which a Victorian music hall performance was staged rather aptly on a Victorian music hall stage. The City Varieties theatre in Leeds welcomed the TV cameras and the wildly enthusiastic audiences, who were egged on by the extravagant words and gestures of 'The Chairman', an extraordinarily theatrical creature called Leonard Sachs.

But up until *The Wheeltappers and Shunters Social Club*, there had never been an entertainment-based show staged in a WMC type setting on the box. 'The Compere' was the much-maligned comedian Bernard Manning, who I knew and worked for in cabaret at his own club on many occasions. I liked Bernard and his attempt at upsetting and causing offence to anybody and everybody really was just an act. The task of impersonating some of the all-time worst caricatures of a WMC concert chairman fell to comedian Colin Crompton. Colin is no longer with us of course, but his daughter Erica is now a successful agent and events producer working out of Blackpool.

Back then the clubs were in-vogue. There was telly on our small screens that the working-class viewers could relate to. With only two or three channels to choose from, the top prime-time shows could attract over 20 million viewers. I chatted recently to my friend Martin Daniels, whose dad, the magician Paul Daniels, was one of those attracting the huge viewer numbers. Martin and I seem to agree that television has now become so terribly fragmented and run by a handful of production companies, booking comedians who started out in the student union bar and who were noticed whilst taking a stab in the trendy comedy clubs. It seems as though the Clubland showbusiness-university-of-life graduates don't get a look in now, as those presenting the overloaded panel shows on telly tend to pick a chum they were 'at Uni' with, to share the limelight.

During the Clubland heydays there was a ladder with rungs to climb. If you could do well in the WMC scene, you could start attracting summer season offers or being offered support slots and an opportunity to work with some of the biggest stars on the planet in the variety clubs, which were also booming. It was the next step up and my ambition when I came into the business was to land a job as a compere in one of these huge pleasure palaces.

By the time I was old enough and experienced enough to run such a venue from the stage, they too had almost all bitten the dust.

Our local variety club was Wakefield theatre club and my great hero, the singer and actor Martin Dale was compere there for many years. Nearby we had the Batley variety club, the Ba-Ba club in Barnsley, the Fiesta clubs in Sheffield and operating as a chain up and down the land. There was the Aquarius club in Chesterfield, where I did manage to work once or twice before it too closed. During this venues heyday, an amazing character called Tufty Gordon, who was to become a friend in later life, ruled the roost as resident compere. In addition, there were clubs such as The Talk of the North and Foo-Foo Lamar's, both in Lancashire, the Baileys club chain, the Purfleet Circus tavern and of course the Lakeside country club in Camberley, Surrey.

The newspapers in any decent-sized conurbation had

many venues to promote and lots of variety clubs and WMCs to choose from. This was boom time and nothing seemed impossible, All the local newspapers had Clubland writers, a revered bunch whose ranks I joined back in 1986. I would continue as a weekly columnist for three local newspapers in my native Yorkshire for thirty-two years.

\*

# 9

# The Clubland
# scribes

With so much publicity required there was bound to be space for local newspaper editorial on the then burgeoning club scene. Local newspapers made a fortune from advertising and some editorial was clearly required to go alongside the glossy, eye-catching advertisements. Finding local Clubland writers who were both suitable and impartial was nigh on impossible. Even if they were impartial, as I myself always tried to be during my time as a Clubland writer, the accusations of bias and favouritism still came thick and fast.

It was often word of mouth that landed jobs on the local newspaper front, and my friend Stan Hartshorne, who printed and published his own Clubland magazine, known as the *Wakefield and District Review*, provided my ticket into life as a weekly newspaper columnist in the *Wakefield Express* in 1987. I went on to produce a weekly column every single week for 32 years. In the end as the club closures piled up, I gave it up, never receiving so much as a thank you after not missing a single deadline since I began. I gave up my local newspaper columns in 2019 and I find it rather odd that no one ever replaced me in the role.

Amongst my regional contemporaries when I began was Roger Holmes, who wrote brilliantly and insightfully for the *South Yorkshire Clubman's Guide*. His column was called 'Oakwell's Spotlight'. In 2017 when I launched the *UK Cabaret* magazine publication, Roger became my first columnist, writing an excellent nostalgia column called 'Roger Remembers'. I was very sad indeed when this kindly and knowledgeable man died in 2019. He was professorial without being pompous and I miss his kindness still.

On the other hand, I could never take to Robin Duke. He was the writer for the *Blackpool Gazette* and in my view, he should never have been let even close to writing reviews on entertainers. He was abrasive and had only an outsider's grasp of how the business actually worked.

The same could not be said of Andy Park, an agent and promoter who covered events around Cumbria and the Scottish borders. Andy even wrote a successful book about the big bands and acts he brought touring into his area. Denis Webb wrote some excellent features promoting many venues in the North West of England and Manchester in particular. So many of these fine writers made their mark and, as is inevitable with those paid to provide an opinion, most were liked and/or revered or disliked and/or reviled in pretty much equal measure.

Looking back, I now feel sorry for Barry Balmayne, who was based in the West Midlands and worked for *The Stage* newspaper, prior to my arrival on the staff there. I remember this hornet-like little man getting up on his hind legs and clambering onstage at The Barn club in Birmingham one evening. While he began his oration with "When I was a scribe at *The Stage*...", Barry was clearly bitter at being let go and regarded his successor (me) with some disdain. After I was sidelined and marginalised by the same company 16 years later, I knew exactly how he felt on that night.

Paul Ford wrote a column in the Yorkshire club programme under the by-line 'Fordi's Flyer'. When he retired from Clubland I was booked to entertain at his retirement party. Fordi was one of the good guys!

Still in Yorkshire and another South Yorkshire Clubman's guide columnist wrote a column entitled 'Here and There with Don Caldaire'. Don liked the young ladies and always seemed to have a scantily clad young woman on his arm every time I saw him. His real name was Albert Heptonstall and using his more glamorous nom de plume must have seemed a good idea at the time.

The *Doncaster Free Press* newspaper employed a musician called Dave Laine as a Clubland columnist for a while. Dave was a great keyboard player/pianist/organist but he could never take Clubland seriously and his column eventually became a weekly piss-take of the activities of certain club committee members, which wasn't what the readers found noteworthy. People in

Clubland don't regard the scene as up for derision, as most of them have been around Clubland all their lives and simply don't get the jokes and the ribbing.

In Wales a lovely man called Derek Wayland wrote columns for a multitude of publications and I liked him very much. Derek just loved the business and when he died suddenly on the day before his favourite annual event, the Showcall Showcase in Stratford-upon-Avon was due to begin, all of his friends just wished for a delay before the arrival of the grim reaper as Derek loved this annual event so much.

Women Clubland columnist such as Pamela Watford and Julie Hodder were very rarely to be found within the pages of Clubland publications or local newspapers. The papers seem to lose much of the advertising base during the 1980s and 90s. It is pretty obvious this was down to club closures, but after the turn of the century, Facebook became the conduit for so much promotion as it is free and those interested in live gigs and entertainment are most usually directed to group sites or the sites of clubs in their respective areas.

The *OC* magazine was once popular with the initials standing for 'Our Clubs' and Sheffield and Rotherham was its target area.

Still in Yorkshire there was the *Club Review*, where a lovely man called Michael Hollaran, based in Leeds, wrote some great copy and was revered by one and all. The magazine still exists today, but its pages are few these days.

*The Entertainer* magazine, based in Nottinghamshire,

allowed club officials to write their own reviews on the acts they booked. Given the existence of nepotism and general favouritism, the resulting trouble was of course both predictable and inevitable.

In the Hull area the long-serving columnist for the *Hull Daily Mail* was and as far as I know still is Dave Norman. I wrote some reviews about his work as compere for a talent show, which he clearly took exception to. I stand by every word to this day and I can say no more than that.

Columnists and reviewers without the proper credentials simply did not pass muster in my perhaps over-critical eyes. In my view, Mr Smith should have never been allowed anywhere near the job of reviewing professional acts for *The Stage*. He would rather write a bad joke about an act than write a good review.

Phil Cook worked for the *Grimsby Evening Telegraph* writing a column called 'Cook's Tour'. Phil was a good writer but it always seemed as though he was carrying emotional baggage, which made his opinions and copy content seem at times erratic and ill-considered.

Les Sutcliffe wrote in the Huddersfield area and his 'Look Around with Les', column was widely read. Les was a good man and a great friend. He was succeeded by Bob Mellor and his excellent 'Rob the Rover' column. Bob eventually became my roadie and I nicknamed him 'Throbber', due to the effect that the malady of gout had on his big toe.

Some columnists were doing the job purely for what they saw as kudos and a bit of beer money. Others did a fine job in promoting what was then a great live entertainment scene. Before me at the titles I wrote for in Yorkshire were knowledgeable men like Jim Daley and Michael St Claire. I was the longest-serving of all the columnists, but that fact in itself may have been a huge mistake on my part. All in all, I had simply endured longer than anyone in trying in vain to promote a scene which was dying piece by piece right in front of my very eyes.

*

# 10

# Understanding the world you just walked into

Yorkshire Television broadcast a sit-com which first aired in 1974 called *Oh No, It's Selwyn Froggitt*, with the eponymous Mr Froggitt being played superbly by actor and former Clubland entertainer Bill Maynard.

The scene was set in a village somewhere in the North of England in stereotypical brass band and whippet country, where an over-zealous and faintly moronic labourer is appointed concert secretary and tasked to book acts for his local WMC. Armed with a mere shoestring of a budget, Selwyn possesses oodles of keenness as he trawls the neighbouring towns and villages in search of talent, encountering lots of assorted oddballs.

The only comparable thing I ever saw on television was the auditions attended years later by Brian Potter/Peter Kay and the hapless members of the committee at the Phoenix club. Incidentally I actually worked at the real Phoenix many times. It was located in Farnworth near

Bolton in Lancashire and is now closed. Its real name was St Gregory's social club.

Bill Maynard himself had worked the clubs back in the 1960s as a singer and comedian, before being cast in a multitude of acting parts, from *Carry On* films to a more regular role as Claude Greengrass in a TV show and 1960s time-capsule called *Heartbeat*. Years later, in the early 1990s I worked with Bill on an ITV series called *Maynard's Bill*, during which we trawled what remained of the clubs that Bill used to appear onstage at.

Back in the old days first-time social club visitors, unaware of the protocol involved in Clubland, must have felt completely out of their depth in the clique-ridden and secretive Clubland world. Outsiders must have felt how a goldfish must feel on the outside of the bowl.

For children coming from a family actively involved in the 'club life', the concepts of community and neighbourhood were just a given. My family were more steeped in the creed of club life than most, which looking back must have skewed my perception of what is actually normal.

My mother was a classically trained musician and was regularly approached to work as a pianist/organist to the acts who visited the local clubs. For whatever reason, Mum wasn't too keen on this kind of work on and had to have her arm well and truly twisted before agreeing to appear. One of the final times she appeared onstage was at Havercroft club, close to where we lived. My dad went with her, but he didn't like the place. More particularly. he didn't care for some of the men who habitually frequented this club, which stood at the side of Cow Lane and next to a housing estate known locally as the Colliery Houses.

The reason for my father's dislike of this club seem to come from his boyhood and a feud between him and a group of brothers who lived in the area and were still frequenting the club in Havercroft many years later. Not too long after Dad started work down the nearby Monckton coal mine at the age of 14, this feud began. I only found out about this very recently and long after his death in 2010.

After the publication of my autobiography in 2020, my cousin Susan duly read the book and was reminded of hearing about Dad as a boy and a dispute concerning the digging up of a school field during the Second World War. The so-called 'Dig For Victory' campaign was brought about by wartime rationing during which every spare piece of land was dug up, with vegetables planted whenever and wherever possible, so that people could actually eat. There was some kind of conflict between Dad and his pals and the brothers from Havercroft and grudges were apparently never settled.

Some disputes festered for years in the old mining communities. Daft stories remained unchallenged with the butt of the jokes or stories becoming sick of hearing about bullshit they knew not to be neither kind nor true. My poor old Dad kept hearing supposed stories from the Dig for Victory disputes and his antipathy to many of the regulars at the club in Havercroft and at the nearby Golden Eagle pub continued for the rest of his days. He would never go near Havercroft club and always advised me to be careful when as an 18 year old I began to visit the pace myself .

Sometimes such tales from the clubs are recalled, recounted and regurgitated by relatives, friends and members of future generations. In the village of Ryhill in Yorkshire where I was born and brought up, I was involved in a huge gang fight, which I mentioned in my autobiography. Perhaps foolishly I omitted to bookend the story with a rather less violent incident which occurred not long after this rather bloody night back in 1982.

I happened to be having a pint in Ryhill WMC, where I was serving on the committee at the time. An old gentleman who I recognised but at that time didn't really know, waddled into the club one afternoon. I was carrying a few bumps and bruises at the time and the mystery man made a beeline for me, opening with a question asking me my name. After establishing my identity, he delved further: "So, are you Frank's lad?" I replied that indeed I was. He continued in the same vein: "So Albert was your grandad then? That means you have to be the great-grandson of Old Tom?" Confirming all of that, the man who introduced himself simply as John, then shocked me by revealing he had in fact known my great-grandfather and informed me, "He was a big, double-jointed man who could still fight anyone right until the day he died . . . And you look just like him. I hear you sorted out a load of idiots outside here last week. I'm not surprised. You are the double of Old Tom and he'd have done the same thing you did and wiped the floor with them."

The story I referred to in my autobiography concerned an unedifying spectacle where I managed to emerge victorious after tackling an entire gang of local miscreants, two of whom ended up in jail after badly beating up and injuring a friend of mine called Rob McGraw, who was left brain-damaged and disabled for life.

I continued to chat to this man John – or 'Big John' as he told me he was dubbed as a younger man – who seemed to be glorifying the violence I had dealt with. Aged just 23 at the time, I was young, fit and fearless with a nasty temper and various belts and qualifications in a variety of martial arts. For some reason though, I have always been uncomfortable around violence and as a result those not looking closely enough at me at certain times have confused my easy-going nature with docility, only to discover later exactly how wrong they were.

John then told me a story that my late father had recounted to me years before. When he was very young, Dad remembered his grandfather (Old Tom) coming to stay at my grandad's house in Ryhill. A group of navvies working on a new road had been terrorising the village and as a result none of the local pubs or clubs would serve them. For some reason Old Tom and my grandfather Albert knew the local policeman, who everyone referred to as 'Bobby Bill'.

The policeman was in need of reinforcements to deal with the navvies and a few local men came forward in the absence at that particular hour of any real policemen. My dad was sent to wake up Old Tom, who was fast asleep on the couch after an afternoon's drinking at the local Ryhill Liberal club. Knowing Old Tom to be of an intemperate and violent disposition when woken too early, my dad, then just five years old and known as 'Little Frankie Boy', was sent to wake up his grandad. The ruse worked and Old Tom was awakened from his slumber and began to play with the little lad. Only when he was fully awake was news of the gang's presence told to Old Tom. Emerging menacingly from behind a huge hedge, Old Tom ably assisted by Bobby Bill and my grandfather made sure the fight didn't end well for the well-oiled navvies. Police then arrived from the nearby village of Royston and the navvies were all locked up. All the men who helped nick the navvies had piled out of the local club and that is how such matters were dealt with back then in pit villages.

My paternal ancestors were horse traders and breeders who must have been backing the wrong horses. Tristram (Old Tom) was born near the horse racing mecca of Newmarket in a place called Babraham in Cambridgeshire. His father William went bust, with three census records revealing a sharp decline in his fortunes. In the earliest census record I found his occupation is recorded as 'gentleman'. In the next census he makes a living as a 'farm bailiff' and in the final census I found my great-great-grandfather on, he is reported to be employed with the intriguing job description of 'railway detective'.

Tristram aka Thomas aka (later in life) Old Tom

worked in a brewery in Burton upon Trent before moving north eventually to start work down Askern colliery near Doncaster in South Yorkshire. Once established there he lived in a building called Lake House and served on a local working men's club committee. The club was set up by miners at the local colliery.

My great-grandfather's first wife had died young and his second wife was a local barmaid who he presumably met at the club, where she worked. My grandfather was the only child from his father's first marriage, but Tristram went on to have three more children with his second wife. When I was a child, my father told me about a large framed photo he had seen where Tristram/Old Tom was posing bedecked with a bowler hat, which was worn at a slightly jaunty angle and resplendent whilst sporting a gold hunter and chain which hung from his waistcoat.

My grandfather Albert always said that his step-mother was very kind to him and he grew to love her. It later emerged that Old Tom and family had engaged in a number of moonlight flits to avoid creditors and other assorted gambling debts.

To give my great-grandfather his full name, Tristram (Thomas) Webster Goodwin died as a result of a seizure, while seated on a park bench next to Askern boating lake. My dad, aged six at the time was on a small boat on the lake and saw the whole thing. My dad recalled his grandad being packed in ice obtained from a local butcher (it was thought that this procedure could restart a heart). Various afternoon drinkers at the nearby working men's club tried to revive him, but he was quite dead.

At some stage my grandfather Albert Webster Goodwin caught religion and subsequently began training as an Anglican priest. A strict disciplinarian with his own four children, he was gentle, kind and generous with his many grandchildren. The piping used to carry the then unchlorinated water made it cold and refreshing when drawn from the tap in Grandad's kitchen and the simple pleasure of drinking it whilst hot and thirsty is a memory which sticks in my head to this day. He died when I was eight and he was laid out in the coffin in the front room, resplendent is some kind of purple-coloured burial shroud. As kids we seemed to be eating anything and everything that was left in Grandad's pantry and one of the items was a tin of sliced peaches. It was decreed that I should gobble them all up with carnation milk on top, as waste was unthinkable. I didn't like them much, and as a result of eating the fruit from a table situated right next to Grandad's coffin, I have never touched tinned peaches from that day to this.

Albert Webster Goodwin never did become a vicar but he liked to tell Bible stories often to us his grandchildren. His religious nature didn't seem to stop his lifelong love of betting on the horses and visiting the local club most days. He went to work down Brierley colliery, until being smashed up in a nasty underground roof-fall in 1935. I was told that betting on a horse provided Christmas presents for my dad and his three elder sisters that year. Dad told me his Christmas stocking contained an orange, some nuts and sweets and a magnificent *Boys' Book of Knowledge*. I own the book today, in which my father wrote in the cover: "If This Day This Book You Borrow – Please Return It on the Morrow. Signed Frank Goodwin age 8."

My dad was not religious at all. He once claimed that the church roof may well collapse on some who went to church on Sunday apparently in the belief their attendance would deflect from being truly horrible people throughout the week.

He did however once describe Jesus Christ as "the world's greatest socialist", claiming that when the Messiah returns to Earth he is bound to approve of the fine community principles which are engendered by club membership.

*

# 11

# Clubbed
# to death

Airbrushed from history, the Great Miners' Strike lasted one whole year and decimated jobs, communities and, of course, the many hundreds of clubs. The miners' welfares were very different to traditional working men's clubs, although many operated on a very similar premise.

The miners' clubs held a fearsome and I believe largely undeserved reputation for being tough to crack for visiting artistes. There were rules for the entertainers to follow, which were never to be found within the pages of a book. For example, many miners did their swearing down the pit, but would never swear in front of their own wives. This meant that comedians visiting the clubs had to mind their language.

The men and their families were often separated in their social lives as they were at work. Men who used the miners' welfare facilities were most usually NUM (National Union of Mineworkers) members. For the colliery supervisors there was often the separate provision of colliery officials' clubs. The officials were underground supervisors and were members of NACODS (National Association of Colliery Overmen Deputies and Shotfirers). It was quite illegal under The Mines and Quarries Act for men to work underground without supervisors who were trained in first aid, gas testing, safety guidance and other skills.

The Great Strike was called in the spring of 1984 when Cortonwood colliery near Barnsley was closed. The then energy minister Peter Walker later revealed that Margaret Thatcher gave him the job over a year before the strike was called, citing her expectation of a strike to come and a resultant and inevitable showdown with the NUM that Thatcher had been planning since she became PM in 1979. With an incentive bonus scheme being rather foolishly accepted in a ballot over two years before the strike, against the advice of the union, coal stocks were high and the previous winter had been a mild one. Thatcher was ready to destroy the entire industry simply because she wanted to and some of the communities remain fractured and in tatters to this day.

There were coalfields all over the UK – from Kent in the South through Leicestershire and Staffordshire, up to Derbyshire and Nottinghamshire, Yorkshire was huge and there was also a Lancashire coalfield, as well as County Durham, Cumberland and Westmoreland, then there was Scotland the old Lanarkshire coalfields, and the huge valleys in South Wales were also a massive contributor to the power needs of the nation.

The working men's clubs and miners' welfares clubs were a nerve centre for the dispute, especially after Thatcher sequestrated the unions' funds, citing her view that the strike which had been called was somehow illegal. Suddenly no union offices existed, other than the national headquarters in Barnsley, nicknamed 'King Arthur's Castle' after the NUM union leader Arthur Scargill. Thatcher had enjoyed plenty of time to prepare before wielding the wrecking ball and Arthur Scargill handled the strike ineptly and naively – in my view at least. Thatcher labelled us 'The Enemy Within'.

Despite being severely injured in an underground accident in January 1983, I remained on the books at Nostell colliery throughout the strike. Still very much involved in the biggest class struggle in this country since the General Strike of 1926 and awaiting a compensation pay-out, I was forced to remain officially a mineworker until the legal stuff was all settled.

During the strike any legal action, such as compensation claims etcetera were frozen in time and I had to wait for my money. I was involved in making money for the strike fund, supporting a campaign which was dubbed 'They Shall Not Starve', which ran a service providing hot meals for striking miners and their families. Thousands of meals were served up, especially after a very welcome donation to the fund by the American rock star Bruce Springsteen who was himself from coal-mining stock. The meals prepared in the kitchens were not for those who wanted them, they were for those who truly needed them.

There was simply no excuse for becoming a scab. Once you went against your workmates, you were damned forever. The depth of feeling remains with so many people to this day. The scab, his family and everyone else around him would be ostracised forever.

I managed to steer the union towards a business-person who was willing to pay for thousands of placards, badges and other such symbols of resistance. The only caveat from the businessperson in question in agreeing the deal was that their identity would never be revealed. We all kept our word.

In times of war, women filled the void left when the men had other things to do and the Women Against Pit Closures movement was born. In today's world of social networking there is a group called 'THE MINERS' STRIKE SITE – NO SCABS, NO EX-POLICE, NO RACISTS OR SUN READERS'.

As weeks turned into months it was becoming clear to Thatcher and the Tory machine that the miners were not about to capitulate. The result was the press, the army, the police, the secret service and the whole mechanisms of the state were soon in place and lined up aimed, cocked and primed in the direction of the mining communities. Resistance proved futile but it was a good fight which just had to be fought. The strike of '84/85 proved to be the last of the great industrial disputes.

My first wife Melanie worked for NatWest bank and was at that time a rising star in the banking union BIFU (Banking Insurance and Finance Union). Affiliated to the TUC, her union were broadly supportive of the miners and her income was keeping us afloat, as my own part-time earnings from the entertainment industry were cut back drastically, with hardly any of the clubs and miners' welfares booking any form of live entertainment. I was running a small, unsuccessful part-time entertainment agency at that time and that made me a bit of an outsider at the pit.

There were other reasons why I was seen by many as an outsider underground, which is a subject I go into in some depth and detail in my autobiography. I was an ex-police officer, who worked part-time in show business, while unbeknownst to me at that time I was suffering from claustrophobia and my best mate was gay. Working down a coal mine, I was hardly going to perceived as popular. Putting all of that aside, I would also proudly say that some of the best men I ever met in my life were encountered whilst working in the bowels of the earth and, although I was pretty rubbish at the actual work and generally very unhappy down the pit, I am still in touch with a few old friends even today. Many of the colliers were great men, hard men but great mates.

Thatcher had managed to bring in her own stooge to manage the strike, a businessman from America called Iain McGregor. He was a destructive strike-breaker with interests in South America. Soon after he had completed the biggest act of industrial vandalism in history, McGregor was paid off handsomely. Bizarrely this oddball American was even awarded an honorary knighthood.

During the strike many of the clubs were used as

meeting places for the pickets, and I remember one night when the comedian Billy Pearce was booked at Grimethorpe miners' welfare club, with the brewery paying his fee and the audience almost all sober, as no one had any beer money. It was a night of laughter, providing respite from the class struggle and the civil war conditions that was literally going on outside the club doors and throughout the coalfields.

On leaving the club after the show I was stopped both on foot and in my car by two men who would not identify themselves, asking where I was going. When I refused to answer, this ridiculously shadowy individual and his silent second-in-command threatened violence and I was ready for action. Only then a commotion broke out down the street and I hopped into my Talbot Horizon car and sped off back to my own home village about three miles away.

I have already mentioned the term 'scab'. There had been hardly any strike-breakers (sometimes known as blacklegs) in previous disputes but eventually the term came into popular use in the mining communities once again. The one basic tenet of trade unionism is that no union member should ever cross a picket line. Most mineworkers in the Nottinghamshire coalfield caved in early and were even subsidised by secretive forces to set up their own breakaway union, the UDM (Union of Democratic Mineworkers). Some of those involved were government-funded infiltrators and quislings, and years later a number of their leaders ended up in jail due to misappropriation of their own union funds. In

Leicestershire the vast majority became scabs and crossed the picket lines. Those who stayed loyal to their families, workmates and communities were so small in number, that the scabs nicknamed them 'The Dirty 30'. This group of men regarded the label as a verbal badge of honour and were soon referred to themselves by this collective soubriquet.

Aside from Notts and Leicestershire, the remaining coalfields were pretty solid for many months, but eventually a trickle of scabs turned into a flood and the strike was lost. So called battle buses were sent to pick up scabs from a pre-arranged pick-up point. They would all then head to their collieries and the police (or at least those posing as police) would congregate complete with full body armour and wielding batons to ensure that the scab buses and the scab lorry drivers hired to transport the coal to the power stations found their way in and out of the pit yards one way or another.

At Nostell colliery, there was a main road which ran past the end of the pit lane. On the main road there was a row of houses in which the miners and their families lived. There was also a brick yard and a nearby quarry. Adjacent to the row there were a few private houses and one of them was occupied by a man who was very popular, prior to the Great Strike. Down the pit he was a mechanic, servicing the needs of a fleet of underground locomotive diesel engines. In his spare-time he used to service the cars of many men from the pit, including my own father's MkII Ford Cortina, registration number GWR 135 J.

It came as no surprise to see him chatting to the pickets on most mornings who were encamped close to his own house at the end of the pit lane. During one morning chat with certain members of the picket line, this man confided that he had picked up some work mending cars at a garage in Wakefield and it was strictly cash-in-hand. His pit workmates wished him well and off he went every day in his own car. A couple of hours later the scab bus would drive through the picket line.

As the days, weeks and months passed, the bus, which was equipped with metal grills at the windows and over the windscreen, held steadily increasing numbers of scabs on-board as they passed and betrayed their workmates. To avoid recognition, some of the traitor's donned masks or wrapped scarves around their faces. All was revealed one day when one of the pickets boarded the bus posing as a scab, pretending he had caved in and returned to work. Once he had taken a look at who was onboard, the picket got off the bus when he stopped outside the pit-head baths, only to be greeted with a handshake from R.R.E. Lewis, the pit manager. Rejecting the handshake, the picket strode back to his mates on the picket line a hundred yards or so away to fill them all in on the identity of all the bus passengers.

At the end of the shift the pit mechanic and the other traitors returned to Wakefield, where they had first boarded the bus. He would then have driven back to his house at the end of the pit lane, where the mood of the pickets had changed somewhat towards him. None of his ex-workmates ever spoke to him again.

Many years later I was involved in a cabaret show at a function room-type venue near Wakefield which was at that time being run by my friend, the cruise ship cabaret singer Vicki Calvert and her husband David. I had known Vicki a long time and she was the person who was instrumental in providing the first opportunities for Jane McDonald to work the ships. Onstage that night, aside from me, was the comedian Jimmy Cricket, who used to be on telly a lot, playing the part of a rather thick and unworldly Irish 'mammy's boy' who had to figure out which feet to wear his trademark wellies on by writing L on one and R on the other. After the show I was caught by surprise when a lady member of the audience asked me to sign her programme from the show. I was pleasant and receptive as I always try to be when mixing with the punters. Only after I had signed did I see that standing right behind her was the ex-scab. The woman leaned towards me and commented, "I think you know my husband." The man stood smiling in front of me. I simply replied that I used to think I did, before turning on my heel and walking off. I just couldn't bring myself to speak to him.

Back in the clubs, just after the strike ended in April of 1985, in an act of lunatic foolishness and elephantine bad taste, a South Yorkshire comedian called Lance Edwards was almost lynched by an angry mob at a club in the pit village of Thurnscoe near Rotherham. The reason for the anger was that Lance, the son of a market trader who sold earthenware on Barnsley market, wrote a parody of a song in which he took aim at NUM leader

Arthur Scargill in front of an audience who had just spent a whole year of their lives on strike. It is hard to fathom this level of sheer insensitivity in search such of an easy laugh. Rubbing your audience's noses in the sheer desperation of the situation they found themselves in, was hardly a way to win friends and influence people who simply wanted to go out and forget their troubles for a while with mates in their local club.

The mining communities had endured striking mineworkers being sacked, illegally arrested and battered by both police and those posing as police with no epaulette numbers on display. A man called Joe Green was run over and killed by one of the scab lorry drivers who was taking his thirty pieces of silver by engaging in rat-runs and delivering coal to Ferrybridge power station near Pontefract.

A broadcaster called James Whale was then a so-called 'shock jock', presenting a late-night radio phone-in show on a Yorkshire station. He incurred the wrath of the mining communities by openly supporting the scabs and others who voiced their support for the government. I knew Whale slightly as I had booked him for some personal appearances in working men's clubs. One night I remember he packed Thornes WMC in Wakefield to capacity. The show opened with singer Dene Michael who found fame with the infamous party band Black Lace, of 'Agadoo' fame. Whale walked on and chatted the packed crowd up, revealing that actually he had no act at all and promptly went down like a one-legged man at an arse-kicking competition. Only weeks later after his

Wakefield appearance, the pit strike began and booking Whale to appear live anywhere would have required a team of bodyguards in order to stand any chance at all of saving him from being held to account face to face by his listeners within the mining communities.

In August of 1984, women of the mining communities started to put up signs on Clubland noticeboards. Hundreds of working men's clubs and miners' welfare clubs asked for women to go out for the day to London in a show of solidarity with their men, who had been on strike at that point for five months. Margaret Thatcher was invited to attend and address the rally and the subject she was asked to speak about was 'The Importance of the Family Unit and Sticking Together'. Many people couldn't afford to make the trip of course, but the clubs helped out by hiring coaches.

20,000 women attended but as they gathered in Trafalgar Square, Thatcher did not accept the invitation and the press and right-wing media completely blanked the event. I was not there that day of course, but the very fact that such a huge gathering of women had taken place at all would have only underlined to Thatcher and her toadies exactly why the National Union of Mineworkers had to be destroyed and the pits closed down at all costs.

When I was employed at Nostell colliery I did a variety of jobs, but I felt like a fish out of water and was pretty unhappy at that time. As I mentioned before, during my final shift underground in January 1983, I was carried out of the pit on a stretcher after a serious accident involving a crush injury. Being above ground made me appreciate how wonderful life could be.

The mining communities were made up of proud people and the clubs that they socialised in were booming for many years. They are all gone now, consigned to occasional examination by those with an interest in what is now known as social history, although memories of strong and supportive communities will live on whilst any of us are still alive who remember the days when Coal was King and, as its knock-on effect, Clubland was truly massive.

\*

# 12

# Selling off the
# family silver

As a newspaper columnist I wrote about the ever-contracting Clubland scene for over thirty years on behalf of various local newspaper titles in Yorkshire. During all that time I simply lost count of the number of occasions when I was asked my opinion of what could be done to turn the tide and stop the haemorrhaging club visitor numbers.

I have thought long and hard regarding the answer of what was the catalyst to social change at that time and I would point firmly in the direction of the sale of council houses, orchestrated again by the Thatcher government. There were also the sales of public utilities to consider too. The social aspirations of folk in the old working-class communities had never previously included the purchasing of stocks and shares. Buying a house was simply out of reach for most, even if it was desirous. Thatcher's answer was to sell the council housing off dirt-cheap to those, like my own parents, who had rented from the council for many years.

We lived on the Mulberry estate in the village of Ryhill and my mother was ambitious and worked hard as a nurse. My parents bought their council house, then a few years later made a killing when they sold it.

Like so many of Thatcher's schemes, the sales of something that technically she or her government never actually owned was great for some, but disastrous for those who sought social housing from within an ever-decreasing stock of council homes.

Society was altered fundamentally in the old heavy-industrial areas during the Thatcher era. Division and conflict were sown, old rivalries were re-ignited and the majority of the Great Unwashed finally said enough was enough with riots breaking out across the UK. Views were polarised, but even the most staunch of the Thatcher fans were beginning to realise the nation was divided as never before.

During the year-long miners' strike, in which Thatcher brought once proud communities to their knees, an IRA bomb exploded in Brighton during the Tory party conference of 1984. Five people were killed and dozens were injured, but this atrocity only seemed to strengthen the resolve of Thatcher's fanatical supporters and emboldened those who were willing to look beyond her increasingly bizarre and unpredictable behaviour.

During this period Thatcher was still revelling in delivering her ghastly Churchillian impression from just over two years before when a small group of Argentinian scrap metal merchants, infiltrated by Argentine marines, raised their national flag on a little-known outcrop of rock in the South Atlantic Ocean. Soon the British-governed islands known as the Falklands were re-taken as an entire fleet sailed in order to turf the invaders off. This undeclared war lasted for ten weeks. The British rallied behind Thatcher, all frantically waving their own flags and apparently consumed with nationalistic fervour and lives were last, battles fought and the British Army emerged victorious. Thatcher, by then under intense political pressure, earned a reprieve.

Margaret Hilda Thatcher, the upwardly mobile grocer's daughter from Grantham, hung on to her job for way too long before finally being knifed by members of her own party in 1990. By then it was clear to most Conservatives that she was out of control, beyond the pale and had finally and completely lost her marbles in the wake of the Poll Tax riots, sleaze accusations and bullying tactics

News of the invasion in 1982 came on the radio one morning and my dad nearly choked on his bread and marmalade as he seemed to be firmly of the belief that the Falkland Islands were somewhere off the west coast of Scotland.

A boyhood friend of mine Dale Richardson was a member of the Parachute Regiment and fought with distinction whilst restoring British rule in our far-flung South Atlantic outpost. A huge street party was held to welcome him home to Mulberry estate and Dale, never as far as I am aware much of a drinker, was treated like a VIP in the local Ryhill and Havercroft social club, where he presumably never had to buy a drink again.

By 1990 Thatcher was gone and replaced by a tedious

grey man called John Major, who had served in her government as both foreign secretary and Chancellor of the Exchequer. Years later it emerged that Major had been cheating on his Tory shires wife Norma with a verbose and patronising Tory junior minister called Edwina Currie, who was frequently prone to gaffes by engaging mouth before putting brain in gear. The mental picture created when it emerged that during their illicit shenanigans the clandestine couple had apparently shared baths together made me and presumably many other people feel vaguely nauseous.

The Tories had flattened the unions, split the working classes and the social aspirations of a generation ensured that club life was simply not in any way appealing to so many as it once was in its 1970s heydays.

The times they were a-changing, but the clubs were not for turning. In 1999 I attended the Club and Institute Union conference for the first time in Blackpool. *The Stage* newspaper was paying me to be there and to report on the big issue at the time, which was that of women being allowed to be full members of clubs. It was claimed by Clubland modernisers that this rule change in itself would be perceived as an indication that the club movement was really ready for the 21st century.

The motion to issue women club-goers with a C&IU pass card required a two-thirds majority amongst the many hundreds of delegates at the annual conference. Over 1,000 delegates entered the Opera House theatre to be greeted by Blackpool's then Lady Mayoress, who addressed the conference before being asked unceremoniously to leave the conference chamber due to the fact that she did not own a penis.

As was the case on that occasion, as it was for many years before and after, the motion was resoundingly defeated. The delegates were all men and many of them had left their wives in the hotels or out shopping, as women were not allowed at conference. I heard many stories of men going back to their long-suffering wives and claiming they had tried hard to allow change and campaigned to allow their women become full club membership rights and had again been thwarted by other male colleagues, who all presumably blamed each other for this annual act of mass chauvinism. They were lying of course and it was not until 2008 when women were finally granted access to the coveted C&IU pass card, which permitted a right of entry to the holders and associate membership rights to any club within the C&IU nationwide.

By then, in terms of appearing to market the social club business in a modern and outward-looking fashion, they were simply shutting the stable door when the horse had long since bolted. Younger people just didn't want to know about the clubs anymore.

*

# 13

# The long goodbye

By the early 1980s, Clubland entertainment had changed beyond all recognition to the two decades immediately before. Already an outmoded concept perhaps, but an additional problem had emerged. The lunatics had taken over the TV asylum and undergrad humour had replaced what went before with the emergence of the so-called 'alternative comedians'. When those running the TV channels go the same university as aspiring comedy chums last seen in the student union bar and at the new comedy clubs which sprang up at the time, the result was inevitable. The old university chums' network is dug in for the long run now. Things don't seem likely to change in terms of the lack of opportunities for comedians in the mainstream, many of whom have chosen to go away to sea and work the theatres on the cruise ships.

The clubs had originally been part of a show business ladder with a chartable progression being both available and attainable for those lucky, ambitious and talented enough to ascend it. The TV talent shows of the days such as *Opportunity Knocks* used to send their spies around the clubs to spot the hot talent. Nowadays Simon Cowell and other opportunist exploiters of the ambitious or the irretrievable stupid film the auditions. What follows is car-crash TV aimed at performers who in the main have no idea how to handle the sudden attention. They have their 15 minutes of fame and are then promptly dropped like a stone.

Back then there was a route in which to acquire the necessary grounding and experience. Initially an aspiring entertainer could try his/her luck at a Clubland audition night. Some areas had their local club federations in which representatives from each individual club could travel to regular auditions nights in which those who aspired to establish themselves on the club circuit could go along and do their stuff. The representatives from the clubs were often dubbed with the title of 'concert secretary'. Then along came the agents, but more about that subject later!

Some clubs began to shut down as working men's club venues and were bought up by local business people. Many of the working men's clubs had fallen victim to the robbers and thieves who have managed to find their way into positions of being left alone to count the takings from slot machines or other such financial fiddles. Committees were elected by the membership. Therefore, if a popular local man who happened to own sticky fingers found his way in, the fiddles were endless. Only when they became too greedy were any of them actually found out.

Many ended up in prison while others claimed innocence and apportioned blame on others. I once found myself in trouble for a joke told onstage one night in a club where the club secretary, who was also a turf accountant, had just been sentenced to some porridge. Without really thinking it through, I announced in jest that the first prize on the raffle would be a month serving on the committee. To my surprise the bookie's wife was unashamedly still using the club and came to give me a piece of her mind about what she saw as a dig at her husband.

Stella's social club was bought up by a glamorous local business couple called Don and Stella Fisher. The club was renovated after serving for years as a community club. From standing defunct and virtually derelict for a few years, the club, which stood in the small town of South Elmsall near Pontefract in Yorkshire, reopened up for business. Don and Stella invited me along as the local newspaper columnist for the area, to the grand re-opening. The year was 1987. Booked to top the bill onstage was the singer Tony Christie, who had enjoyed a great career but, like so many others, his popularity was on the wane by then. Tony did return to fame of course much later due to a certain Peter Kay and his charity release '(Is This the Way to) Amarillo', which was originally a big hit for him back in 1971.

Tony hit the stage along with his live backing band. In between songs Tony had a chat with his audience. Just behind me a group of young women were engaging in a loud and animated conversation. Apparently oblivious to anything Tony was doing onstage, Don Fisher dressed in his DJ and bow-tie marched indignantly over to the women, reminding them that people had paid good money to hear Tony Christie sing and not to listen to their chat. The atmosphere in the room was rather spoiled for everyone as the women refused to belt up and became even louder, before being slung out of the room by the lovely Stella who, despite her elegantly coiffured and regal appearance, was like a bouncer in a bowery. Tony Christie continued onstage but looked crushed by the hiatus in his show. After the show he did not give an encore, choosing instead to leave via the dressing room door, into his car and off into the night. Even by that early juncture in the demise of Clubland it was clear that so many people had no idea whatsoever how to actually be in an audience anymore.

The comedian Charlie Williams bought the former Barber Street club in the small town of Hoyland, near Barnsley which is close to where the classic movie *Kes* was filmed. Re-naming the venue 'Charlie's', this great funny man was still very popular many years after being launched on television by producer Johnnie Hamp is his landmark TV show *The Comedians*. The problems however with such a venue were twofold. Firstly, everyone expected to see Charlie himself onstage there all the time and secondly people were being asked to fork out good money at the door to see acts they could see free of charge at other neighbouring working men's clubs.

By then there were simply not enough stars around that people would pay to see, as the TV opportunities were even then all going in the direction of the new wave of university grad and undergrad 'alternative' types.

The knock-on effect on seaside theatres meant that summer season shows were beginning to disappear in droves, as those popular in such shows were simply from another age. These days only the Pier show at Cromer in Norfolk, the annual offering at Babbacombe theatre in Devon and the shows produced by the great Tony Peers at the Spa theatre in Scarborough remain, with the show becoming the true star attraction as opposed to any individual performer.

*

# 14

# The 'odd-bod' clubs

During more than three decades as a professional entertainer, I have done the lot. Police social clubs, the British army bases in Germany, prison officer's clubs and other works social clubs of all kinds.

I won't name the first police social club I performed in, but my agent received a call from the police officer in charge of booking acts, asking if I performed racist material. My agent sought to reassure this officer of the law that I did not. I arrived at the venue where I was met by this chap. He informed me that "a couple of n\*\*-\*\*\*s will be in with their wives tonight, but don't worry they always go home early, so you can do all your racialist stuff in the second half." For once I was speechless!

The British army bases in Germany followed the model of the UK working men's club, but I always found the sergeants' mess cabaret evenings to be by far the best. No official old-school stuffiness and no junior ranks unruly behaviour. I was once booked at an officers' mess for a dinner to mark the birthday of the Army's Royal Mechanical and Electrical Engineers' colonel-in-chief, H.R.H Prince Philip the Duke of Edinburgh. This was a dinner with a difference as no one was allowed to leave the dinner table once the meal had begun to be served. I had my speech planned but although I tried to prevent my glass being regularly topped up with champagne of a certain good vintage, there was refill after refill. Putting my hand over the glass didn't work as the champagne would simply be poured on to my hand, with yet another glass was promptly pushed before me.

I had been booked by a Sergeant Megram and with a fair amount of the good stuff being already consumed and with brandy on the way, I confided in him that I didn't think I was sober enough to delivered the funnies for 45 minutes. His reply cheered me a little: "45 minutes? You must be joking. All the lads are dying for a piss and after we toast Phil the Greek (the regimental nickname for Prince Philip) we want you to just tell us your half a dozen best stories." I was on my feet less than ten minutes and after a false start when my bow-tie, which was fastened on by Velcro, flew off my neck as in my inebriated state I tried to get up on my hind legs to speak, I finally told my stories. When the punchlines were reached, all I remember is the banging on fists on the dinner table, apparently a sign of their approval. After the dinner myself and my soldier chums repaired into a bar where I won quite a bit of money playing a certain dice game.

As the soldiers then went straight off to their duties, I collapsed into bed and slept like a rock only to be awakened by a vehicle alarm which was going off. It turned out to be my own vehicle which was fitted with an oversensitive wiring system alarm which went off when the wind was blowing too fiercely.

Once way up in Saxony in Northern Germany I was between jobs and heading back down to a base near the town of Munster. The year was about 1991. Myself and my travelling companion came upon the site of the former Bergen-Belsen concentration camp. We walked around for a while and my main recollection was an eery feeling and the complete absence of birdsong. The wind was blowing and the place seemed full of ghosts.

A trip to Thorpe Arch prison officers' club near Wetherby in Yorkshire did not go according to plan as my agent had misread the contract and I was in fact booked to perform for an audience made up largely of prisoners. The prison has an open wing and these particular convicts were just about to be released into the big, wide world. Perhaps after hearing my act, which was awful that night, many of them many have asked to be allowed a further spell of confinement.

The so-called 'Monsters' Mansion' in my own home city of Wakefield once had a prison officers' club actually within the walls, which used to be accessed by a doorframe in the perimeter wall. Wakefield prison, to give the place its proper name, continues to house infamous murderers, sex offenders, terrorists and others deemed too dangerous ever to be released any time soon. The prison officers' club there is a fairly new building these days, situated just outside the prison walls. Its concert secretary when the new club opened was my friend Les Turfrey, himself still a prison officer at that time. Les once told me that the murderer Dennis Nilsen who infamously slaughtered many gay men and disposed of their bodies in all kinds of bizarrely ineffective ways, had once been searched by Les as a matter of routine. Nilsen then reported Les and accused him of sexual assault. It is hardly surprising that once off-duty, the 'screws' like to unwind with an odd bit of gallows humour. One of the bars on the premises is named after the wing which houses all the sex offenders. The door leading the bar has a sign hanging over it to that effect.

I was booked one afternoon into what I was informed prior to the event would be a kind of social club within the walls of the top security Rampton psychiatric hospital. I travelled down to be met at the perimeter gates by a man who helped me set up my equipment on a large and rather dusty stage, behind a set of scarlet curtains. The man asked, "You do know you are performing for some of the patients today don't you?" The look on my face must have conveyed a great deal but the show must go on . . . and it did! The audience were in the main quite appreciative even if a fair proportion of those seated out front would have been certified to be criminally insane, hence the hospital's top security status and its remote location out in the north Nottinghamshire countryside.

Clubs which traded under splendidly outlandish names were common and some of them still remain. I have been onstage at the famed Idle working men's club in Bradford on just one occasion, so I don't wish to speculate on the work ethic or otherwise of the club's members.

\*

# 15

# Where would we be without a laugh?

Growing up, my comedy heroes were Laurel and Hardy, the Marx Brothers and Norman Wisdom. I would later share a stage with Wisdom one night on the Isle of Man, which I went into detail about within the pages of my autobiography.

As a young adult I begin to visit the clubs and experience true live comedy. I had seen comedy performed on telly of course and back in the 1970s there was the opportunity to see all the favourite acts we saw on the small screen out at the large variety clubs, where the big stars of the day would come and play.

During the mid-1980s the demise of venues which I used to visit, such as Wakefield theatre club and Batley variety club was all too apparent. It was claimed at the time by the misinformed folk that the acts had become too greedy and the ticket prices were prohibitive for working people. The truth was that the taxation rates for high-earning entertainers at that time determined their fees had to go up in order to come out with at least some money at the end of the engagement.

For the acts coming up on the WMC circuit, a spot or two on the supporting bill at such venues was another rung on the ladder climbed. There were certainly plenty of such venues during the 1960s and 70s. The Baileys circuit of cabaret clubs and the Fiesta circuit, which including the amazing Fiesta club in Sheffield, a venue presided over by one of the best comperes/presenters and OTT characters I ever met, named Tony Whyte. The Aquarius club in Chesterfield was one venue I myself worked at and the legendary compere, gregarious story-teller and ace musician Tufty Gordon was the man in charge there. In my own home area was the Batley variety club, which was opened and owned firstly by the legend that was Jimmy Corrigan and later on by the hornet-like businessman Derek Smith.

There were a multitude of other venues right across the nation, including The Stardust club owned by the great impresario Barry Young. There were many of the so-called 'Talk' clubs in every area, hence their names Talk of the North, Talk of the Coast, Talk of East Anglia etcetera. One notable survivor amongst the original venues is the Lakeside country club in leafy Camberley, where the owner Bob Potter merits quite a long mention in my autobiography, due to his many quirks and individual qualities in business and as a person. Wakefield theatre club was owned by local businessman Steve Bartle and the agent pulling all the strings at the venue was Bernard Hinchcliffe. The compere was actor and entertainer Martin Dale, who was a police officer during his younger days and who kindly took the time to teach me the ropes in terms of my own aspirations to become a true cabaret compere. In a later chapter I include a list of some of the great venues I myself was pleased to visit.

For comedians, in terms of getting laughs the approach back then was more or less the same, whether you were working on a local social club stage, or if you had managed to climb the ladder onto the variety club scene.

These were the days before political correctness, but I believe there is a popular misconception that all cabaret comedians during the 1960s and 70s were racist, sexist or homophobic. I personally ascribe to the view expressed back in the 1960s by the ground-breaking American comedian Lenny Bruce. He opined that by taking away the offensive words and subjects you only succeed in fuelling the fires of racism and sexism by lending the vocabulary used undeserved power, influence and credibility.

We didn't even know the meaning of the term 'racism' back then. The Race Relations Act of 1976 was long overdue given the abuse and open discrimination experienced by so many immigrants during the 1950s and 60s. I'm not sure how much society was impacting on the inside of individual clubs at the time. After all is said and done, working people visited the clubs to be entertained, see their friends and leave the world outside for a while. Everything seems so grim, earnest and 'over-thought' today.

I can honestly say that I did not hear all that much material aimed at black or Asian people back in the day, although Irish jokes and wife/mother-in-law jokes were commonplace. A new generation of women comediennes began in the clubs during the 1970s and 80s and soon funny Northern women such as Pat Mills, Janice Yorke, Christine Coles, Chrissie Rock and others balanced things out when they themselves went on the attack by criticising husbands, boyfriends and all men generally.

Looking back, I now think that perhaps the whole foul pudding of racism was rather over-egged, with so many mainstream comedians during the 1980s disappearing from view on the telly. My own belief is that so many comedians who pre-dated the alternative guys, were either scapegoated or victims of ageism. The fact is that I rarely heard any racism on the club stages back then. So many funny people were no longer seen on telly and the knock-on effect hit the already beleaguered Clubland comedy scene even harder still, with only word of mouth bringing comedy fans into the clubs.

\*

# 16

# Dying the death

When entertainers work the clubs, we often have to leave our egos at the door, focus and simply take the money and run. In this chapter I hope to explain the feeling of dying inside and how things pan out when it all goes hopelessly wrong at a club gig. In short, the audience and the entire experience can just eat away at a person.

I hope to describe the excruciating feeling of being driven down mentally by audiences which can range from unresponsive to downright hostile. I will follow this with a summary of how entertainers who have just died a thousand deaths in front of a club audience, pick ourselves up off the floor and live to fight another day.

There are some entertainers who won't even admit that they ever experience a poor response from their audiences. There is a term for such people. They are 'delusional fantasists'. End of story!

No matter how talented a singer, how funny a

comedian, how gifted a musician or how personable and skilled they are in front of an audience an entertainer, any entertainer certainly can't win 'em all! I would be both a liar and vaguely delusional myself if I claimed I had never experienced the feeling of a cabaret room full of people who just wanted to see the back of me.

I remember the first death I died just as vividly as the most recent occasion. For me the feeling always manifests itself when I imagine the clocks are slowing or even appearing to stop during my performance. A habit of mine which I have followed since the very beginning is before I even venture onstage, I take a look to see if there is a wall clock in the concert room which will be visible to me even when I am working under the stage lights. When the show is going really well, the hands of the clock seem to fly around . . . but crawl along at snail's pace when it is not.

The sound from the audience varies only slightly when things are going awry. In some cases, they go very quiet and sometimes one kind soul attempts a heckle. The average heckler usually labours under the mis-apprehension that they and they alone are the only one who has ever shouted out whenever inanity they have just shouted. The heckles I have heard over the years range from a simple "get off!" to the old chestnut of a heckle "when's the comedian coming on?" On other nightmarish occasions the audience simply chats over your show. They have become disengaged, disinterested and distant. When this happens, it takes a lot of tricks and techniques and sheer experience to recover and turn things around.

I have heard some entertainers blaming the poor facilities and lack of hospitality in the clubs for their own 'cash and dash' mentality. Clubland dressing rooms can be pretty uninspiring places. Sometimes not only is there an absence of the basics, such as mirrors, coat hooks, or washing facilities. The worst facilities I have experienced have included mould on the walls, vermin scampering around and stacked-up broken furniture, which I have had to test before take a chance and sit upon. Some places are a health and safety nightmare, while others are dressing rooms in name only, as they double up as cleaner's cupboards or kitchens. We can end up jockeying for position between the mops and buckets or, even worse, the supposed 'dressing room' could be a mucky toilet cubicle.

One of the methods I have used to pass the time during Clubland engagements has been reading the often humorous graffiti on the dressing room walls. The connecting doors between the club dressing room and the stage can be daubed with messages all of which have been scrawled on the walls by visiting wags. Legends such as "Christians – This Way to the Lions" or "Abandon Hope All Ye Who Enter Here" are quite commonplace. One of the funniest 'writing on the wall' contributions I ever read was emblazoned in red lipstick on the walls of a club dressing room in Sheffield. It read, "Even the Bingo Dies on Its Arse in Here".

Some clubs used to have amazing collections of publicity photos emblazoned on the dressing room walls. As the new generation of glorified karaoke singers came into the business during the 1990s, there was a noticeable rise in vandalism. The photos on the walls began to be scrawled upon with obscenities or insults.

All of the above facts and anecdotes neatly bring me onto how I developed a long-term survival strategy as a Clubland entertainer. I was keen to do this as throughout my life I have never figured out quite what else I could do to actually make a decent living. I possess no skills or great educational attainments. I have learned all I know by being very lucky. I have met some people who set me up just right when I was a younger entertainer, and their words stuck in my head and kept me relatively sane:

> *The Cardinal Rule:*
> *Never forget that as a visiting act, you are always going to come in a very distant second in terms of what is perceived as important to a successful Clubland evening, Top of the bill will always be Bingo.*

After dying a death, the journey home can be tortuous, especially if it's a long drive. I once died an appalling death at a club in the Yardley area of Birmingham. During the two-hour drive back to Yorkshire I mulled over my deflating experience in Brum. Whilst driving, I thought of the stage, the band behind me, what I did wrong, where I went wrong and what I could've, would've and should've done. Too much navel-gazing. I have learned to try to put a bad experience right to the back of my mind and move on quickly.

On another career low point, I worked at a club in Keighley which contained probably the most hostile and out of control drunken audience I ever played to. A club in the Kirkheaton area of Huddersfield was nightmarish for all kinds of reasons and actually transformed me from being an easy-going, 'get on with anyone' type of person, to a downright nasty piece of work. Clubland can do that to you.

The challenge in terms of keeping mental health problems at bay as an entertainer is to be able to close the door and drive away at the end of the night, simply closing the whole experience out of your mind. You draw a line. You move on.

In order to retain one's sanity as a Clubland entertainer, the rules are simple and there is a magic formula which applies to absolutely everyone:

1. *Turn up on time.*
2. *Be as polite as possible.*
3. *Know your act inside out and deliver it the best way you can.*
4. *Take the money.*
5. *Go home and forget all about it.*
6. *Look forward – don't look back.*

At the beginning of this chapter, I mentioned that I remembered my first ever death and my most recent. My first was way back in the early 1980s at a greyhound club near Pontefract. The most recent was in 2018 at a football supporters' club in Alfreton, Derbyshire, where the folks just hated me and I went down like a knackered lift.

Almost 40 years have passed between those two very similar experiences and what have I learned?

I have learned to remember the wise words of Kipling, (that's Rudyard and not the cake-maker): "Meet with triumph and disaster and treat those two imposters just the same."

Whenever I do have a particularly bad night in front of a Clubland audience, I still hear the words of my first agent Les Parker ringing in my ears. He himself was a great all-round entertainer. Les once advised me: "In Clubland remember the seventy per cent rule. If you are being offered rebookings at individual venues seventy per cent of the time or more and you have a bad night, don't worry, it's not you, it's them!"

\*

# 17

# The nearly
# men

I have never wanted to be famous. I really should make that abundantly clear right from the start of this particular chapter. That fact alone goes a long way to explain why I have managed to stick around for so long.

I had seen the ugly side, which manifests itself when some show the sheer levels of ambition and subsequent desperation by the lengths they are prepared to go to and the depths they are willing to plummet to in order to climb the greasy pole of show business. You are only as good as your last show and no matter who the entertainer is willing to flatter, deceive, bribe or sleep with, nothing will change the fact that toughness and talent are the two prerequisites for those who wish to stay afloat in the shark-infested waters of the entertainment industry. I have known people to be consumed and destroyed, starting with their souls and spreading like a poisonous fungus due to either alcohol or drug abuse, or often by developing mental health problems.

Fragile confidence, self-esteem and other factors such as body confidence and bad vocal technique can all conspire to make even battle-hardened entertainers adopt a fight or flight posture.

I can only imagine what the singer and musician Kevin Kitchen must have been through. Kevin left the clubs during the early 1980s to become a pop star, only to return to the Clubland stages after being unceremoniously dropped by his record label, after his debut single barely scraped into the Top 20 and the others barely charted at all.

I would dearly love to throttle the smarmy and obsequious Simon Cowell and his 'judges' who are invariably more famous than the people they claim to have discovered. They build people up who have no idea how to handle their 15 minutes of fame and then watch gleefully as they subsequently and almost invariably plummet down the pecking order as quickly as they came.

Their treatment of the superb entertainer Ricky Kay by the Cowell machine was nothing short of scandalous. In any other generation of show business Ricky would be an enormous star, as would others such as the brilliant comedienne and ultimate all-rounder Siobhan Phillips and a multitude of others kept off our TV screens simply for being perceived as 'too cabaret' (whatever that means)!

Young singer Peter Grant had started as a guest of my own in some Clubland shows. His first album *New Vintage* climbed into the Top Ten of the album charts.

His second album bombed and young Peter faded quickly back into obscurity. Peter has lived and worked all over the world since then but only ever found that one big chance of fame.

My friend Ricky Graham took the opposite journey. Ricky was a teen idol as a member of the 1970s chart-topping band Child. His real name is Graham Bilborough, which was the name he was known by whilst famous and appearing regularly on *Top of the Pops*. Suddenly it all came to an abrupt halt, so changing his name to Ricky Graham, he launched himself into the clubs as a solo singer.

Graham/Ricky is a natural entertainer, but I often wonder what the change of pace must have felt like. Not long after going solo I had arranged for him to appear as a glassworks social club near Barnsley. Also on the bill was a comedian and magician called The Great Soprendo. I chatted to this portly man of magic for a while and was introduced to his partner, who had accompanied him on the night. Only much later did the penny drop that I had been up-close and conversing with Victoria Wood.

This was about the time she was appearing on the consumer-based current affairs TV show *That's Life*, with Esther Rantzen. Victoria seemed quiet and rather diffident but as she helped her partner (real name Geoffrey Durham) to pack up his props, I had observed Ricky/Graham returning into the club, after doing his own disappearing act during the magician's spot. Ricky arrived back just in time to perform his own spot onstage but his temporary absence caused a bit of sweating on the night for the club chairman. I heard only a year or so later that this stress-head club chairman had suddenly dropped dead as a result of a sudden and huge heart attack.

Four lads from South Yorkshire formed a band called The Gents and looked to be heading for the big time. The lads, Martin John Burton, Steve Chambers, Glynn Davies and Steve Kendall had written some great songs and augmented their self-penned song set with mod-style covers, during the height of their popularity in the clubs back in the mid-1980s.

The Gents were jointly managed by Paul Burton, a very quiet and sincere chap and the brother of one of the band members, and a fascinating character called Bill Wright, who ran a business-savvy company called Bankhouse entertainments. Bill's offices were in the village of Holmfirth, on the very streets where the Yorkshire geriatric sit-com romp *Last of the Summer Wine* was filmed for so many years.

The Gents were waiting to be seen by the right record company, who would light the blue touchpaper and launch them. Their debut album was actually entitled *Waiting to Be Seen* and I was a huge fan of their music. Their songs ranged from a punchy track called 'The Faker' through to a fun-twist on the music of Henry Mancini called 'The Pink Pantser'. My personal favourite track from The Gents was a delicate guitar-based ballad called 'Something Happened'. In the event, it never happened and the band eventually broke up, their artistic hearts collectively broken.

During the beginning of the Covid nightmare, The Gents' bass player and lead vocalist Martin John Burton cheered me up no end on social media by playing his guitar and singing all manner of covers via Facebook. Many of the songs were his own and those that were not penned by Martin he made his own. Such talent!

But what did it feel like to actually venture onstage during those Clubland heydays? The atmosphere in so many clubs was electrifying, with many established artistes being kind enough to pass on their knowledge and giving valuable advice to younger fledgling performers, as believe it or not I myself once was. I remember kindness and guidance from comedians such as Jimmy Marshall, Bonnar Colleano and Bobby Diamond, who had been part of a hit variety act called The Diamond Boys.

Those Clubland stages were hallowed ground to those of us who had grown up within the whole Clubland vibe. We were walking where the show business gods had been before us and the pressure to cut the mustard broke so many of us. A breezy air of confidence and a strong element of being able to bluff it a bit certainly helped so many of us. Having egos battered sometimes produced strange behaviour. I'm told that back then I seemed arrogant and aloof to so many people. I look back on those days with great regret, but my only excuse for my behaviour was that, albeit subconsciously, I was merely building and maintaining my support system. Skin as thick as that of a rhinoceros and selective hearing often came in very handy whilst performing in the clubs.

Some entertainers took mates or family members to ride shotgun at the gigs. Often family and friends of entertainers went along as 'roadies' or even 'sound engineers', twiddling knobs, adjusting vocal effects and pressing the play button on an array of various backing track sources.

I made few true friends, remaining cautious of those who followed me around from club to club. Stan Hartshorne was a true friend and helped me in and out with stage equipment for many years until his death from lung cancer.

I worked way too much, chasing the short-end money and the local gigs, but somehow eventually I began to climb the fees ladder a bit from 1990 onwards, with the following seven years seeing me being forced into the VAT bracket due to my high business turnover.

I consider myself extremely fortunate that I managed to plot my route into regular Clubland work, firstly as a singer, by finding a few role models whose authority and advice I would never even question. I was helped by great entertainers such as Peter Wallis, Johnny Dawes, Les Parker, Martin Dale, Patti Brook and in particular by Derek Armitage and his accompanist Trevor Tunnicliffe.

Since then, I have either enjoyed or endured a few brief and fleeting bits of high-profile success, during which times I have most usually made a complete dog's breakfast of things.

Perhaps it's a form of vertigo. As entertainers we seek approval and when we receive a degree of praise and recognition after being placed on a pedestal, we take a look at the view down the mountain we have just ascended and our heads wobble, causing us to take a fall and be forced to start all over again.

Brickbats and bouquets are one thing of course, but there are those who, susceptible to flattery and full of hopes, dreams and dripping with egocentric fervour, become easy prey for the 'hangers-on'. These are normally showbiz junkies with no talent of their own, who seem all too eager to build the artiste up and then take such great pleasure in knocking them back down again.

I have never considered myself anything more than a journeyman professional entertainer. I am well capable of raising a laugh or two and can hold a tune. All I ever ask for is a modicum of respect, which I feel I have earned over the years and a smidgeon of recognition for simply sticking around for so long and never actually being out of work for any length of time . . . until the arrival of a global pandemic.

I have made some enemies over the years, most notably club-goers in my own home area, who saw and read my views on all things Clubland in their local press every week for over thirty years. Some of the more mean-spirited amongst them would be openly hostile to me on the few occasions that I found myself booked into a club close to where I lived and continue to live to this day.

Some of my fellow entertainers have taken umbrage with me over the years, but I won't name and shame any of them here. After all, they seem to mind me a lot more than I mind them. Wearing two hats in Clubland was tough, mainly due to the fact that I only ever displayed one face to the world.

The danger from the entertainer's point of view is that some find trouble switching their stage persona on and off. Once the show is over, many entertainers struggle to come out of character, and the simple acts like going around the shops and maybe being recognised here and there can create friction for the wives/husbands and families of Clubland stage performers. I hadn't been living with my Bevvy for very long when we were engaged in a shopping exhibition to buy kitchen appliances, and suddenly whilst in negotiation for a good deal with a shop assistant, I started turning on a bit of onstage Mark Ritchie-type cheeky patter. Bevvy said nothing at the time, but quite rightly took me to task later on. I explained to her where my odd behaviour had sprung up from and I tried to make sure it never happened again.

While none of the Clubland acts are exactly famous these days, we are recognised a lot in the streets. Those who stare are usually trying to figure out where they have seen you before. The trick is not to make eye contact and speak only when spoken to face to face, especially if someone calls out your name from across the street. I have seldom appeared on television over the years and only sporadically at that. I'm willing to bet it is strange for the truly famous to be forever picked out in a crowd. Although these days, the ordinary people with no talent in Reality TV-land are the high-profile people now while the talented people sit at home or are themselves busy making a living out there entertaining live audiences.

The Clubland entertainers these days are in my view much less professional than those of yesteryear. The reason is of course is that many of them simply aren't truly professional in a business sense, with a combination of day jobs and an all-too obvious lack of grounding determining that their motives for being on the stage can range from satisfying the whims and fantasies of pushy parents, to simply generating extra income.

So many of what remains of the few club stars out there today have managed take the 'show' out of show business. Hardly any of them dress appropriately for the stage. A very wise man once told me that stagewear should be defined as "looking different to the members of the audience". These days many audience members look smarter and better-presented than the people to come to listen to. Worse still, I often see entertainers who walk around out front and sit in the audience between their sets in the same stagewear they have just been donning out onstage.

In my view many of them are glorified karaoke singers who seem to have very little idea how to interact and engage with a live audience. Singing along to backing tracks seems to be the limit of their ambitions and aspirations, which is pretty sad in itself. I doubt very much whether many of the few new club stars coming through would last five members in front of the audience which packed the clubs during the heydays.

Today all that remains for entertainers in so many of the clubs which continue to plod on in business in the 21st century, is to sing or perform to small crowds of folk, the majority of which have probably only come into the club in the first place for a game of bingo and a grumble.

In some cases, a significant number of today's Clubland entertainers have simply been late starters, who seem to use the entire experience to embolden themselves, often to tackle issues such as low self-esteem, or to please a pushy husband or more usually an overbearing wife. The penny drops eventually with some of them that perhaps they are not as talented as they or their partners once thought they were. Sometimes after just one too many knocks to their confidence, some disappear punch-drunk and confused, vanishing from the Clubland scene as quickly as they came.

*

# 18

# Naming legends

Some of the names which follow in this chapter will mean nothing to most readers, aside from those who remember the heydays of Clubland. What follows is me simply listing my own Top 20 acts and entertainers that I either saw and loved, or worked with on one or more occasions.

The list below is in no particular order, and I have thought long and hard on who would be included here. It's just a personal selection of my own. The acts listed evoke either happy and/or personal memories. Maybe my list will contain the same names as many from my generation, who remember the days of the true club stars,

Those bygone days when the crowds of eager punters would form a queue before the club was even open, in order to secure the best seats are now only a distant memory.

The club-fillers were club-fillers for a reason. They had honed their craft and knew the business inside out.

Here below is my personal Top 20 club-fillers.

**1. Dukes & Lee** — Simply the best Clubland act I ever saw. A married couple who presented an exhausting confection of comedy, music and dance. The Dukes & Lee show featured members of their own family within the framework of their brilliant act. Ronnie Dukes, small, tubby and bespectacled, found fame late in life and died as a result of heart trouble before he could really enjoy his life at the top of the profession. His glamorous wife and stage partner Rikki Lee, also now sadly no longer with us was a lovely singer and a truly great straight woman. Their older children played in their backing band, with Rikki's mum becoming the perfect foil for Ronnie's barbed comic insults which she feigned ignorance of whilst seated at the piano. Simply the best.

**2. Harry Parker** — An all-round entertainer who filled clubs for many years. Harry earned a fortune and people used to queue outside waiting for clubs to open, just so they could get to see the great man in action. Harry lived in a caravan and never seemed to have any money. After he retired from the stage around 1975, he went to work in a bakery in Barnsley. Harry died largely forgotten in a residential home in his hometown of Barnsley in 2000.

**3. Paul Shane** — Paul worked in the pits before going onstage full-time as a singer and comedian, after recovering from a serious back injury which he sustained at work. After finding fame in the hit Perry and Croft TV comedy *Hi-de-Hi!*, Paul moved up a few notches but was always interested in the club scene. Just before he found fame as camp comedian Ted Bovis, I was offered him by an agent called Bill Smith for a show I was booking acts onto. To my great shame and embarrassment, I turned him down and a few short weeks later Paul was a household name.

**4. Dave Betton** — My biggest influence as a young entertainer, I went to see Dave many times and I found his impressions, his comedy stand-up and his superb singing voice to be a revelation. I had no idea that one man could possess so much talent.

**5. Marti Caine** — A great showbusiness lady from Sheffield who performed comedy superbly and could also sing. Marti endured a tough life and suffered a great deal. She found fame and wealth but died far too young.

**6. Mighty Atom and Roy** — Mo Moreland found fame as a member of Les Dawson's dance troupe The Roly Polys. Long before that, the diminutive Mo and hubby Roy were filling clubs and joking, singing and tap-dancing in front of massive Clubland audiences.

**7. The Meers Brothers** — Two lads from Chesterfield who played a bewildering array of musical instruments and even managed to coax a tune out of a variety of everyday objects and household implements, such as kettles and hose pipes. This was true variety and these brothers were one of the first truly great Clubland acts I ever saw during the 1970s.

**8. Burnette** — I mention Burnette, or Howard Burnette to give him his full name, at length in my autobiography. Howard was a one-off. Uniquely zany and funny as any comedy magician since his hero Tommy Cooper. I miss Howard still.

**GIL RAY**

*Vocal/Inst/Entertainer*

Representation:
**LES MORGAN VARIETY ORGANIZATION,**
**VARIETY HOUSE,**
**BIRDWELL,**
**Near BARNSLEY,**
**SOUTH YORKSHIRE.**
Telephone:- Barnsley 81166 & 86920 (STD 0226)

**"BOOKING THE BEST IN SHOWBUSINESS"**

**9. Gil Ray** — A language teacher by day, but by night Derek Gilruth transformed into multi-instrumentalist, singer and comedian Gil Ray. All his jokes seemed to begin with the same comedic preamble "So there were these two skinheads in Barnsley . . ." I was his agent for a while. I liked him and he liked me.

**10. Billy Pearce** — As funny as they come, Billy started as a dancer, taught by his dance teacher/choreographer mum and has been around the stage all his life. Billy is a pantomime legend and has been as big a victim as any of the policy of putting on only university-educated people on telly in light entertainment. Billy's star still shines brightly. I am proud to call him a friend and I'm sure that, whilst he still has breath in his body, Billy Pearce will always be a laughter-maker and spread more than a little happiness.

**11. Huff and Puff** — When this highly camp comedy act, presented by two heterosexual entertainers, broke up, someone quipped that "Puff went off in a huff because Huff went off with a puff". Due to changing times, shifting sands in comedy and of course more PC attitudes, this act wouldn't last five minutes today but back then they were funny as hell! During their act, when Huff asked Puff if he had had any sex lately, Puff replied that he had been to the local shop in order to purchase Vaseline and they were out of stock. The shopkeeper asked if he had tried Boots? Puff replied, "Boots? I want to slide in, not march in!"

**12. Peter Wallis** — Nicknamed 'Machine-Gun' due to the speed of his delivery, Peter was a special friend of mine and had a great influence on my own early efforts to entertain people. Peter worked with everyone, from Ronnie Barker and David Jason to The Grumbleweeds when the band were at the height of their fame. Peter was a funny man and a decent man. I wish he was still around so I could enjoy another lovely chat with him.

**13. Johnnie Casson** — Perhaps the most imitated of all the stand-up comedians who came out of the Northern clubs and a great man who should have been a much bigger comedy star than he eventually became. Johnny was a drummer in band called The Cresters, but the comedy took over and the laughs have never stopped since.

**14. The Discoes** — A comedy mime act who were professionalism personified. The members of the act were also entertainment agents by day. By night they simply mimed to the hit songs of the day, whilst engaging in knockabout comedy and quick-change routines. You really had to be there! One time I saw them at Lundwood WMC near Barnsley when halfway through their act, a fistfight broke out at the back of the room. One of the members of the act was Rex and he asked for the house lights to be put up before engaging in a sort of comedy boxing commentary, as he watched the inebriated pugilists set about each other. The combatants finally twigged what was going on and promptly dropped their fists, burst out laughing in unison and soon they headed for the bar wrapped in the sort of embrace which the Spanish refer to as 'amigos para siempre' (friends for life). Order was restored and the show continued apace.

**15. The Gents** — I mentioned these Yorkshire lads earlier in this story and my abiding memory of them was when the band appeared at The Farmers club in Kinsley near Pontefract. I was just recovering from a major underground accident in the coal mine where I worked for a time. I was covered in bruises, cuts and other injuries and I had a plaster cast on my broken leg, but somehow, I still ended up on the dance floor with the aid of crutches.

**16. Dragonfly** — A superb live band who were announced onstage behind the tabs. When the curtain went up, a toyshop was revealed onstage. The toys came to life in the shape of five musicians who sang and played some of the best and catchiest covers of the time. Magical!

**17. Rag and Bones** — This Bradford-based comedy duo made me laugh perhaps more than any other act. They are pictured here during the stage version of *Hi-De-Hi!* with actress Sue Pollard, who played Peggy Ollerenshaw, the chalet maid and wannabe Redcoat in the show. The lads never got a break, but the memories linger and thinking of these boys always makes me smile, even though the last time I saw them on a stage was probably around 1981. I always remember the boys onstage in the mining village of Fitzwilliam, between Wakefield and Barnsley. It was New Year's Day and there was a pea-souper fog outside which was so thick that traffic stopped. I had gone to the gig by bus as it was only in the next village to where I lived at the time. The buses were stopped, which resulted in a three mile or so walk home in the fog for my first wife Melanie and myself. Despite the freezing fog, we laughed all the way home.

**18. The Zimmertones** — Two boys and one short-lived career in comedy before one half of the act, Mike Craft, went to join the hit-making band Smokie. Their time together was tiny, but their talent was huge.

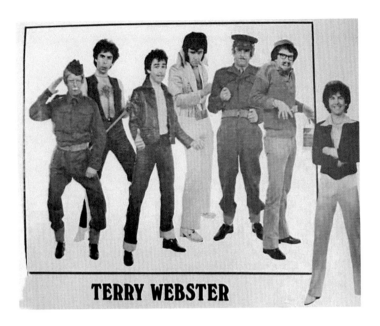

**TERRY WEBSTER**

**19. Terry Webster** — A spectacularly talented musician, songwriter and comedy impressionist who has done the lot! Formerly frontman of the hit comedy band The Rockin' Berries, Terry was one of the last of the old variety club headliners and he found fame involved in the 1980s novelty chart hits released by the studio band known as Jive Bunny.

**20. Tony Wayne** — My best show-business friend. Those who have read my autobiography *Right Place... Wrong Time*, will know exactly why we are so close. A great singer and entertainer with a kind of cult status in his day, Tony has been a classic fool over the years, giving away much of his wealth to charity or to a selection of assorted waifs and strays who infiltrated his life and frequently abused his trust, his friendship and his innate kindness. Tony was born in the next mining village to my own birthplace and although I still insist that he has been foolish during much of his life, I myself have been an entirely different type of fool.

I really must give honourable mentions to a few others.

I loved the flamboyant pianist Mike Terry and the singers Paul Somers and Michael France were both class acts. Comedian David Copperfield seemed set for stardom in a BBC series called *Three of a Kind*. The other two members of the comedy cast were Tracey Ullman and Lenny Henry. Somehow it just didn't seem to happen for David on telly, but he was an incredible live act. The comedian, musician and hit songwriter Sammy King is right up there on my memorable list alongside comedy duo The Barton Brothers, stand-up comedians Jimmy Carol and Roy 'Slither-Man' Jay. Keith Davidson was a true vocal entertainer. And, last but by no means least, I want to mention the great Stan Richards, a pianist and comedian who later found fame as an actor, playing the poacher Seth Armstrong in the rural soap *Emmerdale*.

So many acts, so many memories, so much joy and laughter.

\*

# 19

# 'We must curb the artistes' agents'

When I first became aware of all things 'Clubland' I remember reading a newspaper article penned by a man called Jim Daley. This Yorkshire-based Clubland columnist warned about the power that he thought was being wielded and misused by a new brand of entertainment agents that sprang up during the 1970s.

Due to the lack of expertise on entertainment matters within the ranks of most club management committee members, it was thought that agents should be given booking control or sole booking rights of individual clubs. As a result, the club would receive a list of the forthcoming attractions every month, as well as often glossy and eye-catching posters to put on the club noticeboards. The club secretary or treasurer would also receive a monthly bill, which listed the fees of the visiting acts. If the club booked bands or more expensive acts, the bill could run into many thousands of pounds a month.

The agency business rapidly became big business, with

a combination of ex-entertainers and eagle-eyed opportunist business men trying to persuade the gentlemen of each individual club committee that they alone held the power and possessed the necessary influence to service a club's live entertainment needs. Convincing often naive and unworldly committee members was a piece of cake for smart alec agents, but there were also some of the more unscrupulous committee members who wanted their piece of the action.

Back in the day in post-war Britain, as the variety theatres began to fold, clubs began to book all manner of live entertainment. Most of them appointed someone from their own ranks to act as booker and resident 'expert' on all live show and music matters. It didn't seem to matter one iota that the chap in charge may have spent his working week down the pit or emptying bins. When the weekend came, he was 'Mr Entertainment'. Besides the lack of knowledge, a basic eye for the main chance was the driving force for many as soon such club men were on kickbacks from agents, and some acts even offered a piece of their fee to the concert arranger in turn for a booking arranged complete with an inflated fee.

Such men had different job titles throughout areas of the UK. In Scotland they were known as 'social convenors', in many areas they were simply known as 'ent secs' or entertainment secretaries. In Yorkshire they were invariably dubbed with the title 'concert secretary'. The early successful Clubland agents, using the ones based in Yorkshire as an example, were Johnnie Peller,

Slim Farrell, Ernest Johns, Gordon Kellett, Les Parker, John Wagstaffe, Al Crossland, Palma Joyce, Bill Turner, Steve Jackson, Derek Franks, Owen Hammond and Les Morgan. The one thing they had in common was that they were all very sharp operators and presumably made an awful lot of money during those halcyon days.

Outsider agents who represented their own stable of acts were effectively kept out of certain clubs controlled by rival agents. This was accomplished by the use of something called the 'swap system'.

Aspiring entertainment agents had to be granted a licence by the Department of Employment when I applied to launch my own fledgling agency in 1979. All licence applications appeared in the then hallowed pages of *The Stage* newspaper on a Thursday. I was granted licence number YH788, which presumably meant there the 787 agents in Yorkshire and Humberside who had set up before me. My registered office was the small back bedroom at 63 Station Road, Ryhill. The sheer volume of mail arriving by the Saturday morning after my licensing announcement appeared in *The Stage* was massive. The postman brought it all in a separate sack to my house.

These days *The Stage* is in my view merely a London-centric theatre paper, but back then light entertainment people nationwide used to read it, receive coverage in it and of course advertise their wares in it. *The Stage* was the newspaper for all the entertainment industry. Alas not anymore.

On that Saturday morning I had just done a night shift down Nostell colliery and when I eventually awoke from my slumbers, my then wife and I began to sift through oodles of fliers, photos and miscellaneous publicity material in the days long before email. A new agent attracted a flood of publicity which was all dropped though my letter box. I remember those offering me their services including a zany looking and rather elderly magician called Crisco a comedy scriptwriter called Cardew Robinson and stand-up comedian Dick Pleasant, who promised me he could deliver "Comedy all the Way".

Not long after I began to dabble at trying to become a fully-fledged agent, I discovered that the trade body known as the Entertainment Agents Association (EAA) was in open conflict with its members in Yorkshire. As a result, the Yorkshire Agents Association was launched and rather bizarrely I was almost immediately elected as its vice-president.

Many of the Yorkshire agents had been taken the task for introducing and subsequently mis-using something they dubbed 'the 'no-pick system'. Back then it was most usual for visiting artistes to be paid on the night, either by cash or cheque. Many of the agents were having trouble obtaining their commission (which could be anything between 10% and 25% of the gross fee). Some agents simply asked the clubs to send the money for all the visiting artistes at the end of the month. The agents then simply deducted their commission and sent a cheque for the rest of the balance due to the artistes.

After a few years it became clear that some agents were using the money as false cashflow by hanging on to the money for way too long and only releasing it to the artiste when they really had to. As a means of countering this, in 1997 the government made this illegal and the artistes' money had to be held in separate clients' accounts.

Another scam committed by some unscrupulous agents was to send the club a bill for an artiste's services of, for example, £200. The artistes went along and performed the gig having agreed to work for a considerably lower fee. The agent would then take a commission on the £200 and simply pocket the rest. Those of us with a little nous checked what fee we were supposed to be receiving on the night. I actually caught one agent red-handed in this illegal act.

The legal relationship between an artiste and an agent is a simple one. The artiste employs the agent to represent them, who agrees in return to pay a pre-arranged commission on everything they earned. The agent decides which acts they want to represent and which they do not.

Many agents began to act in a high-handed and irresponsible way, which is kind of predictable when there are large sums of money at stake I suppose. The lines within the business relationship became blurred with agents claiming, "He/she works for me." Some both then and now see themselves as the employers or the bosses of the acts they represent. Sometimes it needs to pointed out to some of the more egocentric types that it is actually the agents who are supplying a service to the artistes.

I look back at those days and I often think how much interest was earned by rogue agents who seemed to forget who actually went onstage to earn it in the first place. Most played by the rules but a significant minority managed to mix their own money up with what by rights belonged to others, and the die was cast. Meaning another nail in the Clubland coffin had been knocked in.

Bizarrely the Tory government of John Major completely deregulated the agency business and its activities. Agency licensing was removed and a whole new generation of part-time cowboys and crooks moved in on the action. By the 1990s Clubland needed new agents like a stray dog needed another flea.

*

# 20

# Anger is
# an energy

Anger is an energy or so they say. When I was young, I was hungry for success and when I did not achieve my aims, that made me angry. If energy is fuelled by anger, my energy levels must have dissipated with age. I seldom become angry these days. Anger is just too exhausting.

Looking back to 40 years ago, I was angry. I remember becoming very angry during a committee meeting I had been invited to at Ryhill Liberal club. It emerged that the club concert secretary Horace Peers and club secretary Dick Vincent had only invited me to tell me I was not going to be supplying the club with acts anytime soon. This to me smacked of an act of grandstanding, performed by people who had an exaggerated sense of their own importance simply because they happened to be wearing the badge of office worn by club officials.

I had supplied the club with great acts such as The Zimmertones, Walk and Windy and others, but the fly in the ointment was a comedian who went by the name of Mr Moses. A band had let me down at the eleventh hour for a Saturday night gig at the club and during the summer, replacements were hard to come by. The agent I was working with at the time was Owen Hammond. He sent along Mr Moses and I was actually in the club watching in horror as he walked off without raising a single laugh, or any kind of applause at all. I took the credit when the shows went well and the blame when they did not. That was the deal.

I was angry after a committee meeting held at Grimethorpe WMC during the pit strike. The committee had invited lots of agents to pitch their services for the booking rights to the club. A number of us turned up and saw the committee in turn. All of us bought the dozen or committee members a pint each. The other agents could probably afford this, but at the time I was a striking miner too. The gentlemen of the committee were never informed of and I never revealed what my day job was. I became angry when I later learned through the grapevine that the agent Bill Turner was in on the ruse of the committee to obtain free beer from all these rich agents. Bill had known in advance that it was he alone who would be providing the club with acts going forward.

Clubland was already shrinking when the pit strike hit, and it was the start of the beginning of the long goodbye as some clubs became private venues while others closed as a result of the criminals and their committee fiddling. The crowds were starting to become older and were not being replaced by their own children and grandchildren in the clubs.

Then along came the national smoking ban, which from an entertainer's point of view produced an audience which suddenly became a moving target as the 'Charge of the Light-Up Brigade' headed for the doors in order to feed their addiction in a variety of hastily erected 'smoking shelters'. Before the smoking ban was introduced in 2006, it was simply an occupational hazard to find ourselves performing in often badly ventilated concert rooms, where the acrid smoke would sting our eyes and scar our lungs. On arriving home, when it time to hang up our sweaty stage clothes, all we could smell was second-hand fag smoke.

Some bands and acts supply their own lighting rigs in order to make the whole thing more of a show. They augment the lights with the use of so-called dry ice machines. Whilst appearing with such an act in a double-bill just before the smoking ban was implemented, the members of the duo were taken to task in the dressing room by a club committee member for using dry ice during their opening set. They were told in no uncertain terms not to use it again. The irony was that I could have cut the cigarette smoke in the unventilated club with a knife. It was like a dense pea-souper fog, yet the smokers did nothing but complain about the harmless substance being used onstage just to make the show look better.

I have travelled the world over the years and realised that our social and leisure market is light years behind the rest of the world, as I discovered during a trip to

Australia back in 2007. In the Land Down Under they don't have working men's clubs, they have 'RSL' clubs. The abbreviation stands for the Returned and Services League of Australia, and the clubs are involved in similar work as is conducted by our own Royal British Legion.

Along with Bevvy and our friends Baz and Sue Smith, who emigrated to Australia and started a new life just outside the city of Brisbane, we witnessed first-hand how the Aussies do it. The clubs are lit up like Las Vegas casinos and offer plush restaurant facilities as well as gaming casino rooms, lovely lounge bars and sports rooms. All of which is topped off by the 'bottle store', which is what we would call an off-licence. The supermarkets in Oz don't generally sell booze or use cheap tins of beer as 'loss-leaders'. This adds a great deal to their licensed sector and also ensures that, unlike this country, young binge drinkers are not usually already drunk from home consumption before they hit the town.

Today in 2021, Clubland in the UK is full of part-timers and portfolio people. It is very difficult now to make a living these days as a professional entertainer. Those days are gone. There are no television opportunities or other types of exposure for ambitious artistes. There are no acts capable of filling a club simply on their own name any more.

*

# 21

# The
# K-word

A very wise man once told me that once you let the audience onto the stage, it is all over. The magic is gone. The mystery and glamour viewed from the audience's side of the lights was once respected and the proprieties of how to conduct oneself as an audience member were instilled, mainly by those who ran the clubs during their heydays. Then along came karaoke.

The Japanese phrase meaning 'empty orchestra' was coined by tired Tokyo businessmen who wanted to find a way to wind down after a day of working in the big city. Who could have known what the effect of singing to a machine in a bar could have held for mainstream show business as we once knew it?

From the point of view of those running social clubs in the early part of the 1980s the introduction of backing tapes constituted the thin end of the wedge. Prior to the invention of backing tapes, live music ruled. Singers had to learn how to work with a live band or have written musical arrangements produced to enable them to work with resident backing musicians who, up until that point were employed by most of the clubs. In many cases, just an organist and a drummer would be up there onstage. For the visiting cabaret artiste, the standards of musicianship ranged from quite superb to extremely patchy. Some organists were great at reading arrangements – until their view of the music became clouded in alcohol.

As solo artistes in the clubs, many of us bought cassette decks to play the tapes through. The backing tapes, or tracks as they became more popularly known, varied hugely in quality and another factor was the quality or otherwise of the often-bulky PA systems that we entertainers lugged around from club to club. Back then the Clubland acts could work every night if we wanted to. There was a living to be earned and the clubs were usually full.

Somehow Clubland entertainment lost its soul and the whole thing became empty, with singers spending half their spot leaning over and adjusting their equipment as they sang along to their backing tracks.

Suddenly many of the great Clubland stages began to look huge, with a solo singer or entertainer standing there and twiddling to try and make the sound coming out of the speakers acceptable to the audience and with not a musical instrument in sight. Many punters complained about what they perceived to be loud but tinny recorded backing music hurting their ears.

It is seldom even mentioned that inviting audience

members on stage is fraught with difficulties. Public Liability terms and conditions, in most cases, determine that once a performer, or even a karaoke presenter, invites someone on stage, he/she becomes responsible for the safety of the audience member. If they trip, fall over something or even fall off the stage, solicitors are often swiftly involved.

Some of the club committee people liked the changes wrought by the so-called 'self-contained-acts'. It meant of course that they no longer had to pay the backing musicians. As ever, not being business people, the committee members knew the cost of everything but the value of nothing.

*

# 22

# One for the boys
# and then the girls

When I was still in my teens a group of lads asked me to join them for a Sunday lunchtime drinking session in a local working men's club. I was promised that I would have the opportunity see 'a bit of exotic'. Either I was naive or stupid, but I honestly had no idea what to expect.

The club in question was in the village of Shafton near Barnsley. This dormitory mining village was famous or at least notable for one thing and one thing only: the Shafton workshops. This complex was a massive source of employment for many hundreds of local craftsmen and it was owned and operated by the NCB (National Coal Board). Much of the equipment used underground in the coal-mining industry in this country was either built or maintained at these workshops. As there are no more mines, there are of course no more workshops, no more jobs of that kind and no hope of much in the way of meaningful employment for a whole generation of

Barnsley kids, who don't want to work in a call centre, a warehouse or behind the counter at McDonald's.

Returning to the 'bit of exotic', it soon became clear that naked ladies were going to be a key part of the entertainment and the venue was Shafton Green WMC. The exotic reference was revealed by a stag comedian who also acted as compere for the day and his meaning in describing the women as 'exotic' was simply another way of saying the performers were both black women strippers.

I don't remember too much about the show, other than one of the lads in the audience took the opportunity to peer through an open-door jamb after the show. He watched surreptitiously as the women were getting dressed again, which struck me as rather odd given that he had just seen them onstage only moments before completely naked and posing in so many ways.

For some of the young teenage lads, this would have been the first time they had even seen a naked woman. After the show we all headed off to walk in the direction of a club in the village of South Hiendley which stayed open later and quite illegally at that time, but some of us were always welcome to enter by the back door. As we left to start the ten minute or so walk between the two villages, we passed a car in the car park in which a small black boy was sitting in the back seat reading a book and eating crisps. At that time black people were seldom seen in the area, so no prizes for surmising that the child's mum was one of the women being lusted after onstage.

Later the Shafton Green WMC club went bust and the

building was bought by the Clubland singing star Derek Armitage. I knew Derek for a while and this fine singer simply had his accompanist Trevor Tunnicliffe onstage with him while Derek invited guest singers on to the stage. This was one of the first venues I ever sang publicly in. By then the place was known as The Singing Man.

Women's rights seemed to rise higher on the Clubland agenda after the miners' strike was lost and the steelworks shut. Many of the old industries were adversely affected by our close association at that time with what later became the EU. Germany kept their coal and steel industries, while in this country our politicians allowed us to be effectively enslaved and, in my view, conned into becoming a low-skilled service economy.

This was underlined by the hit film *The Full Monty*, which was released just as club closures began to spiral, which seemed to resonate with so many folk at the time. Much of the male stripping action in the film was shot at Shiregreen WMC in Sheffield. The club is no more, but the legacy the film left is one of collective appreciation of proud men who once made steel and simply wanted some semblance of self-respect.

*

# 23

# The big
# shows

The slogan 'As Seen on TV' was often seen on the
noticeboards of many Clubland venues during the
1970s and 80s. Back then someone who had enjoyed a
bit of telly exposure could fill a club on their name alone,
whilst at the same time pulling down often eye-watering
fees.

Brewery roadshows were big business and the 'suits'
at the breweries used to turn out in force to create
flagship events in which they could maintain and
nurture business relationships with individual clubs. The
huge barrelage orders from the clubs generated big
discounts, which were sometimes passed on to thirsty
club members at the bars. Live cabaret entertainment
was key and very soon circuits of clubs were visited in
turn by some of the most high-profile acts within the
individual areas. All of which was paid for by the
breweries.

I was lucky enough to find myself booked into a few

different brewery-sponsored roadshow events and the work created a big income stream for me, and for once I was finally a bit of a name in Clubland.

I remember one show very well indeed, in which the top of the bill attraction was Eric Delaney and his big band. Eric was billed as 'The World's Number One Showman Percussionist' and his albums sold very well in the charts to those who enjoy the big band sound. We toured around so many clubs and Eric and the gang were great company.

Already a septuagenarian back then, Eric was as fit as a butcher's dog and his drum kit actually revolved around the full 360 degrees during the mother of all drum solos as his act came to its natural crescendo in the finale. On telly at that time, a popular advert in which many drinkers of Carling lager engaged in a multitude of difficult tasks created the slogan 'I bet he drinks Carling Black Label'. Much to the delight of the brewery roadshow audiences, as Eric's drum riser revolved, the slogan was revealed, emblazoned in huge lettering around the drum kit Eric was playing so expertly.

Eric and his original big band used to star in the big variety clubs. By the time I met and worked with him, Eric had put together a smaller band and was doing the club brewery roadshows. Near the end of his life, I saw Eric working alongside a keyboard player in a late-night cabaret bar in Benidorm.

I always thought that Eric Delaney must have loved show business very much to be willing to shrink his show down to match the level of the business he had found himself in. The great man had appeared in three Royal Variety shows during an illustrious career. He had albums at the top of the charts and was universally admired within the business. Eric Delaney died in 2011. He was in his late eighties and played on until the end of his life, mostly performing back in some of the clubs where his career began.

Show producers were often agents with a grounding onstage and great clubmen like Les Parker in Yorkshire and Jim Tait in the North East of England were just two major figures who spent years of their working lives bringing big live shows to the masses in Clubland.

The Blackpool Command Show is an annual event which is organised and presented to coincide with the weekend of the Club and Institute Union conference in Blackpool every April. The original intent of presenting this show was to reward artistes with lucrative Clubland work on the Fylde coast. I was chosen to appear in the show in 2000. I had never secured much work in Blackpool before my appearance and things didn't change for me after my appearance.

Blackpool Clubland these days is a sad, sad place. There are still some nice club venues, such as the Hotels and Apartments club for instance, but most of the great venues are now gone forever. A very nice club man called Alan Pilborough tries very hard to keep the whole thing going via his continued support for a magazine publication called *The Seasider*. After Covid and at the time of writing, I'm not sure if there will be another Blackpool Command Show. I hope there is. It is a great flagship Clubland event which was always held for many years at the Horseshoe Bar in Blackpool Pleasure Beach.

Supposing there is another Blackpool Clubland Command Show, I'm not sure if that would be an indication that Clubland is still alive and kicking, or if it would be simply a futile exercise which would be simply forestalling the inevitable?

\*

# 24

# What happened?

Of all the great variety clubs, only the Lakeside country club in Camberley, Surrey, still remains open for business. All of which made me wonder what became of all the old cabaret playgrounds where the big stars used to come and play. This chapter contains a list of some of the great venue names and reveals if the buildings are still there or not.

The venues I mention here were all either true variety clubs or the larger and better-class working men's clubs, which so many older people still remember and cherish the memories of. Here are just a few of the venues I visited:

**Aquarius Club, Chesterfield** — Compere Tufty Gordon was the man in charge and the club lasted longer than most. I think I may have been one of the last artistes to appear there, as I was booked for a Thursday, Friday and Saturday night run alongside a pop group called Tanya Tevaro and Session.

**Ba-Ba club, Barnsley** — Once owned and operated by a stage hypnotist called Peter Casson, the Ba-Ba sank without grace and became part of a huge town centre redevelopment.

**Baileys circuit** — Many venues operated under the Baileys banner up and down the UK, but the difference between these plush nightclubs and other independent operators was that they signed artistes up to be exclusive to their venues only. It was a bold move at the time but it paid handsome dividends in the early days, with even supporting artistes gaining their own individual Baileys followings amongst the regular cabaret fans.

**Batley variety club** — Now a gym and health club in the old mill town of Batley, this club was a flagship venue when the superstars of the day came to play. From Louis Armstrong to Shirley Bassey, from Morecambe and Wise to the great American singer-songwriter Neil Sedaka, who I saw at this venue one evening back in 1976, they all came and the crowds flocked to see the stars. Following the Fun Pub route of the early 1980s, the club was rebranded as The Frontier and some great live bands came to play. My friend the showbusiness tailor Neil Crossland put a charity show on, featuring some of the stars who had graced the stage many years before. This was in 2010 and it marked the last time the club resembled its old self in any way. The lingering question I always find myself asking when I chart the end of the great clubs is doesn't anyone want to dream anymore? Surely the public can't be interested in the reality TV people forever.

**Belle Isle club, Leeds** — The old club was razed to the ground by fire back in 2000, but a new club emerged like a phoenix from the ashes a few short years later. The club secretary these days is Peter Fletcher. I recently labelled Peter the most patient man in Clubland as he deals calmly and dispassionately with the moans and groans emanating from some of the club's members on their Facebook account. It is great to see this club still running, but I can't help but think back to appearing at the old club, where the backing band was led by a rather spiky and acerbic musician called Tony Cervi.

**Dialhouse club, Sheffield** — I worked this club many times, backed by the resident band which was led by the great organist Terry Herrington. The club was allowed to close in 2010 and I appeared in a large-scale charity concert there, just before this huge Clubland pleasure palace was cleared to create room for yet another housing development.

**Embassy club, Harpurhey, Manchester** — This club belonged to comedian Bernard Manning and if ever a man was given a bad press it was Bernard. I used to work there pretty regularly and I found the experience of meeting with and working with Mr Manning to be completely at odds with the terrifying descriptions of him which I had read about in the press. I can say no more than that!

**Fiesta club, Sheffield** — Part of the circuit of clubs up and down the country, the Fiesta club stood right in the city centre and I saw Sheffield's own singing star Tony Christie there on one glorious night out. He was introduced onstage by a wonderfully flamboyant compere. His name was Tony Whyte and the man was a complete one-off and a mass of contradictions in the shape of one elegantly dressed performer. His stage presence was rather aloof but yet in private he loved to give help and advice to aspiring artistes. This expansive and learned cabaret entertainer chatted and gossiped away garrulously, but it was a well-known fact that he never spoke behind anyone's back.

**The Fun Pubs** — When some of the great variety clubs began to close during the early 1980s, some adapted and became known as 'Fun Pubs'. Bar staff were armed with tambourines and in-between pulling the pints they joined in with the tunes. A Dutchman and his boyfriend, known to one and all simply as 'Keis and Philip', bought up old club premises in Huddersfield, Barnsley, Leeds and Wakefield and some great nights were had by mainly younger crowds, who enjoyed top bands such as Helen Day & Wild Affair, Stagefright, Dragonfly, Bitter Suite, Pinkertons Assorted Colours, Jimmy James and the Vagabonds and so many, many others. Wakefield theatre club became the Pussycat fun pub and I seem to remember a barmaid who worked there who liked to sing. Her name was Jane McDonald.

**Greasbrough club** — In the interest of accuracy I should point out that the original club was partially demolished and adapted more than somewhat to accommodate a supermarket around 1980. The new club is further towards the edge of the old part of Greasbrough village near Rotherham. As comedian Les Dawson observed in his own autobiography, the boss at Greasbrough was a man called Les Booth who booked all the stars, from Jayne Mansfield to Bob Monkhouse and made the most of the old gambling laws in his pursuance of illicit wealth.

**Jim Windsor's club, Leeds** – Later known as Les Parker social club, this city centre venue was a magnet for talent scouts, agents and club officials from right across the area. I never met Jim Windsor, but Les Parker who bought the club around 1976 was my first agent. Like so much of the city centre of Leeds, the buildings of this venue are no more, as the area became subsumed into a new shopping development. As the Leeds-born Alan Bennett once observed, Leeds doesn't have much of a visible past as those in charge seem to knock it all down every few years to make way for something else.

**Kettlethorpe WMC** — on the edge of a housing estate between Leeds and Wakefield this really was a venue which quite literally went from boom to bust. A man called Frank Parker ran the place and, according to some, allegedly ran the place into the ground. The club was still pulling huge crowds right until the end and the reasons for the closure remain a mystery to this day. The area the club once stood in is now a student accommodation living complex for those studying at the nearby Bretton college. On my final visit to the club, the Paddy Green Set were onstage. This was a group led by a mad comedy Irishman who really was a one-off. The place was packed, but only weeks later it was boarded up. The venue was then re-opened and re-branded as The Kettledrum by a

Yorkshire businessman called Tommy Wickham. I worked there in cabaret many times.

**The Mecca circuit** — Later rebranded as Tiffany's clubs, these venues were lavishly appointed dance halls, but the stage facilities were simply magnificent. I first visited the Mecca in Wakefield just as it was about to be rebranded. Every male customer had to wear a tie and at ground level the huge dance floor gave way to a huge revolving stage. On one side, the resident pop group Kentucky Blue used to play for dancing, until it was time for cabaret, or often a guest band who began to play just as the stage revolved and the visiting attractions came into view. Upstairs they were other nooks and crannies, including the Kon Tiki lounge, where revellers could dream of relaxing on South Sea islands whilst drinking cocktails from imitation coconut shells.

**Oceans 11 Club, Manchester** — Now a supermarket, this fine club provided a touch of class within the bustling great Manchester club scene. Driving past one evening, I wondered if the people who now operate their shop business within the venue realise that this was a place where the stars used to come out and play every night.

**Stardust club, Bardon, Leicestershire** — Owned and operated for many years by show business entrepreneur Barry Young, the Stardust was briefly home to the then world-famous Showcall Showcase. This shopwindow-style event was produced by *The Stage* newspaper and there was a good vibe around the place. A businessman bought the old premises and the place now functions as an Asian shopping centre.

**Wakefield theatre club** — Now demolished and serving as a sports stadium car park, I was invited in just after the venue closed (by then known as the Pussycat) for the last time. There was talk for a while of a local businessman called Harry Tranter opening the place up again as a variety club. All I can say is whoever was in charge of the venue once it became defunct can't have been too careful who they gave the keys to, as the old premises, which had hosted everyone from Michael Jackson to Howard Keel, had been plundered and looted by a group of local chancers. The premises later became home to a bowling alley, before being demolished completely in 2015.

**The Talk of the Coast club, Redcar** — Right of the end of its business life, I was booked to appear at this club as a supporting artiste to a very well-known female singer from yesteryear. Arriving early, I barged into the dressing room only to discover the aforementioned singer, skirt hitched up and bending over the dressing room sink, whilst receiving the full undivided attentions of a young man who was firmly 'in the saddle' with his trousers around his ankles. I made my apologies and left, only to return later in time for the show. This famous lady, by then upright again and fully-clothed, explained that she was "helping the young man with his singing career". I couldn't help laughing!

The venues listed above and so many hundreds of others are all gone now but certainly not forgotten. Not by everyone. The clubs listed were part of the lives and careers of so many performers, some of whom went on to become stars. These clubs also provided a rung on the ladder for acts who had ambition and were willing to learn how to handle the bigger stages and the expectations of the more discerning audiences. These were just a few of the many and appear here due to the fact that I visited all of them, either as an artiste or as a member of the audience at one time or another.

For the patrons, such venues lived long in the memories of people who just wanted to be entertained by performers who knew about true live music and wanted to learn their craft.

For some, the big variety clubs provided an extra special night out, seeing stars they were only aware of through television and enjoying facilities which they had previously never experienced.

My own 18th birthday was spent at Wakefield theatre club, where the bill included the magician, Paul Daniels. Paul's son Martin Daniels works the ships with his own cabaret act these days. I once told Martin the story of seeing his dad onstage that night. Paul had learned his craft and *The Paul Daniels Magic Show* was a primetime BBC Saturday night show once upon a time, when the show regularly attracted audiences of around 20 million viewers. I happened to be in the town of Whitehaven in Cumbria one evening back in 2001 whilst representing *The Stage*. Paul Daniels was appearing in a kind of one-man show. During the first half of the show Paul, ever the consummate professional entertainer, performed a mesmerising display of classic tricks and illusions in his own inimitable style. The second half of the show I found even more interesting, as Paul conducted a Q&A session with members of his admiring audience.

He began to field all kinds of questions, but the one that made my own ears prick up in interest came from a chap who asked what Paul thought of *Big Brother*? I expected Paul to go on a rant about what was wrong with 21st-century telly and how we should return to putting talented people on telly and letting the so-called 'ordinary people' watch and enjoy at home, instead of juxtaposing the whole process and making the talented people sit things out at home and watch on in horror and disbelief as certain types of so-called ordinary people are invited to pick their noses and navel-gaze on the small screen.

Instead of that, Paul's answer to the question was a classic. He replied, "I watched it once and I thought, ho-hum!" I'd say "ho-hum" just about sums it all up, from the youthful and vacuous flesh-flashers of *Love Island*, to the idiotic fading stars of *I'm a Celebrity*, all desperately keen to remove the last bit of shine on their fading stars by consuming horrible insects in Australia.

The knock-on effects of reality TV are many. Below are just a few:

> There is no way for young and talented music creators to play and be heard.
> There is no show business ladder to climb, resulting in no stars with no talent being created.

There is no mode of training, rehearsal or preparation who those who truly do possess the X-factor.

There is a whole generation of entertainers who found themselves in the right place, but at the wrong time.

There is no hope for so many splendid young 21st-century performers, who in any other generation but this one would be enormous stars on television.

There are no guides or mentor figures to help or give advice to up-and-coming aspiring entertainers.

There is no show, so there is no show business.

Television is with a few notable exceptions ho-hum. It comes – it goes. I generally find television highly educational, as every time someone turns the set on, I go off and read a good book.

From the point of view of the relatively few live entertainment venues which remain today, the question is who do they book and put on their stages? There is no one famous enough to sell the tickets and no one seems to know the value of talent these days, only the cost of that commodity, which is an entirely different matter.

Those who are receiving the telly exposure are often Oxbridge graduates or other similar university graduates, who make money by touring and booking theatres for one-nighters. A very high proportion of today's comedy audience members are themselves university-educated

18-to-30 type people. Everyone else is ignored and former live entertainment devotees are left disenfranchised.

It is no coincidence that so many theatre dates are planned in university towns and cities. It's sort of like comedy for those with a certain IQ. So often audience members find themselves looking at each other during shows, seemingly in order to figure out whether the comedian's material is meritorious or clever enough before they decide whether or not to find it funny.

There is no variety on television. But not because people don't want it. The true reason is that no one has the depth/breadth of knowledge or wit and wisdom required to actually present it properly and decide what actually constitutes 21st-century variety. No one in Tellyland knows how to do it.

Television is in itself split into a hopeless schism. On the one side we have the Oxbridge graduate telly producers, who fall into the trap of trying to entertain whilst simultaneously attempting to 'educate' the viewers. Some of the panel shows, of which there is a real dearth, are more like lectures on campus or at best seminars in the student's union bar. On the other side of the coin, for those who don't necessarily possess the intellect required to actually follow what is going on in student-politico land, there is reality TV. For the irretrievably stupid there is of course Keith Lemon.

The result of all of the above is that most people sit at home being spoon-fed the sickly confection they choose to chuck at us, the Great Unwashed. The Oxbridge mafia are firmly dug in nowadays, so there will be no chance and no hope for variety or those who learn their business on Clubland stages.

I love to go out and see live comedy and some of the most popular 21st-century exponents of stand-up. Eddie Izzard has in my view moved stand-up comedy forward by light years. Jim Jeffries is incredibly clever and funny as hell. Mark Thomas is intense and funny at the same time. Although I don't always understand what he is actually doing, I still find Stewart Lee unmissable. Lee Mack and of course Peter Kay are the only comedians I see with universal appeal, across different age groups and what are now referred to by those who love to pigeonhole as those in all the socioeconomic groups.

At the same time, no live stand-up has made more laugh more than Billy Pearce. Bernard Manning had the best delivery of any live stand-up I ever saw or worked with. Cannon and Ball possessed the quality of warmth and togetherness onstage, even though for many years of their career Tommy and Bobby simply did not get on very well. Some of the best stand-up comedians are now making a living on the ships, with Rudi West, Gareth Oliver, Herbie Adams and The Man They Call G immediately springing to mind, despite being scandalously overlooked by the Oxbridge cartel.

The clubs are falling like ninepins, as those who run them really have no idea what to put on their stage which may just conceivably drag a few people in through the doors. The majority of the comedians who do telly wouldn't be seen dead on a club stage. Instead, they find their audience and their level for simply hiring out theatres which happen to have a university campus nearby.

A few years ago, I was booked to perform on a Tuesday evening at Sheffield Lane Top WMC, which is a very well-appointed club situated unsurprisingly in Sheffield. A musician who was resident at the club told me that the week before my appearance, a camera crew from an independent television company had turned up with a big comedy star and asked if they could film the club and its members. The aforementioned big comedy star went around asking many of the bingo dabber-wielding Tuesday night regulars what made them laugh? One of the best responses came from a bloke who served as the club concert chairman (in charge of stage lights and so-forth). His reply was that, in his opinion, "the best comedians tell us jokes and the worst of the comedians we see on telly seem to want to just swear at us and talk down to us." I think that was a fair point well made.

The big-star comedian then ventured onstage and started to talk *at* the audience, who in the main ignored him and watched in a sort of semi-detached kind of a way as he floundered around and started to take the piss out of the club, the audience and the world in general. I went on just one week later and made them laugh, but you very rarely see me on telly. I looked on the famous comedian's Wikipedia page, which unsurprisingly revealed that he was educated at Cambridge University. I myself was educated, to an extent, in Grimethorpe, South Yorkshire. He graduated with a 'first'. I graduated with a black eye and a huge chip on my shoulder.

We come from two entirely different worlds, but the world I come from holds no power or influence in television-land and neither do the acts who work the few remaining clubs any more. The world of academia is well-catered for on telly. The world the majority of us live in is sadly not.

The sales of the cheap supermarket loss-leading cans of beer serve at least to deflect people away from the sober thoughts of managing to pay the mortgage every month and living in their bubble, bringing up kids and then waiting to die.

When I was growing up, there were only two and then three channels on telly, but very often families didn't bother with it at all. We played games, we visited each other, we engaged with and tried to help our friends and neighbours. Virtually at the end of every street there was a club, a miners' welfare or some kind of live entertainment venue where we could go along, enjoy the talent onstage and, for some of us at least, we could learn about show business and maybe even dream a little.

*

# 25

# What future?

As I revealed in *Right Place... Wrong Time*, I had a bit of involvement in the early career of Jane McDonald. I used to know Jane quite well, but I haven't seen her to chat to for many years now alas. We have a mutual friend in singer Sue Ravey, who appears in some of Jane's telly programmes even today.

During my entire time spent in Clubland, Jane McDonald is the only entertainer who, steeped in the creed of Clubland, clambered out of the show business trenches and attained true stardom. Famously of course she did it by trotting expectantly up the gangplank of a certain cruise ship just at the exact moment when a BBC film unit were engaged in the production of a series all about cruise ship entertainment, *The Cruise*. A bit of luck for Jane certainly, but well-deserved nonetheless.

Jane managed to secure useful contacts (I was one of them) and she cut her teeth as a performer on the Clubland stages. We had the same agent for a while. In fact, it was I myself who introduced Jane to the man in question.

Since then, success has followed success and, despite a few Clubland types using social media to vent their bile, vitriol and jealousy towards her, I say good luck! Jane proved to be the exception to the rule that even non-Oxbridge types can be successful in television in the 21st century.

The sad fact is there haven't been any more like her. By that I mean of course entertainers who have paid their dues and done the hard miles as a Clubland entertainer. Jane is a one-off and while I am so tickled pink by her success and I have been for many years, I can't help thinking her one-off status is such a shame. There is so much talent out there who, like Jane, have paid their dues but are shut out by those who don't recognise rehearsed, prepared and/or natural talent such as that which can be found on the admittedly fast-diminishing number of Clubland stages, even today, every single week.

I have developed friendships, some long-lasting. with so many great Clubland people. Keith McIntyre, a great Clubland concert secretary and one of the most talented, artistic and truly gentle man that I ever had the pleasure of calling a friend, springs to mind. Bryan Winter, who taught me a great deal about C&IU matters back in the day and Jim Tomlin, who developed dementia way too young and was a huge loss to Yorkshire Clubland as an administrator and a champion of new talent are all high on my list. Last but by no means least, I must mention a dear man called Fred Horton, who I have so many lovely memories of his kindness and humanity. They are all dead now, but my life and the lives of so many others are richer for having known all of them.

The once great Clubland empire is ultimately doomed. There are no stars created and the people who once flocked to enjoy a live show night atmosphere in a club are, at best, getting on a bit, with most of them shuffling off their mortal coil and headed for the great bingo game in the sky.

There are some splendid young people around today, but technology has determined that so many of the young coalesce around the immediacy of the electronic age. Mobile phones and social media which have created reality TV and a generation of inward-looking, self-absorbed, self-entitled robots, who rarely engage with others or socialise in any recognisable way. Instead, so many of the young use the 21st-century tools at their disposal as a diversion and as a prism through which they peer at the world, whilst pickled in their own narcissism.

Will the great days of brotherhood, sisterhood and neighbourhood return? I think not. When the last game of bingo has been played and the last singer has sung their final 'false-tab song', someone will then close and lock the last club Clubland concert room door and turn off the stage lights forever.

The great Clubland empire was mainly fun while it lasted. Time now to turn the page . . .

*     *

*

# *Acknowledgements*

I am grateful to Adam Press for the cover design and to so many people who offered access to their collections of Clubland memorabilia.

I would like to thank Tony Wayne and Julie Johnson for being on hand to help me spot the mistakes and of course to my Bevvy for her patience and love, as I read the material to her out loud and ad nauseam as I seek her approval chapter by chapter.

I also wanted to thank Jo Speight for her continued encouragement and so many people for their kind words about the first book, all of which encouraged me to move on quickly and produce this second volume.

I also thank Martin Brown for his continued technical help and support.

Friends and supporters who were also encouraging included Lisa Pearson, Jackie Hanson, Sue Ravey, Ronnie Ravey, Lindsay Emmitt, Julie Marshall, Valerie Mann, Tanya Walker, Mark Aston, John Smyth, Cathy Summers, Danny Andrews, Cathy Usher, Mike Hainsworth, Shaun McGilloway, Andy Greaves, Peter De Loriol, Barrie and Vicci Lucas, Nathan Downes, Graham Bardsley, Stewart Masters, Claire Jones, Khadija Noor, and Beth and Jan Hurley.

I was also grateful to my agent Tracey Gunney and all at Ricky Graham Leisure and to my legal eagle Jennifer Aspinall.

In this my second book I tried so hard to avoid my entertainer's nature, which may have seemed to some as though I was somehow pushing myself to the front and taking centre-stage in so many of the stories. At the first time of writing, the early part of this book did not resemble the finished item very much. Bevvy persuaded me that my stories, told first-hand, were the reasons why so many kind readers praised my first book *Right Place... Wrong Time*. Taking all of that onboard, I rewrote quite a lot of material in recognition of Bevvy's advisory mantra that "the best stories all have you in them".

I used to think that writing the book and actually getting everything down on paper was the hardest part. The rewrites, oversights and amendments are the parts which make the steam fly out of my ears.

I definitely want to thank so many kind friends at my local pub in Normanton near Wakefield West Yorkshire. When the first book came out, I gave a copy, as a present, to my great friend, the pub landlady Maggie Mills. Instead of passing the book around and taking it in turns to borrow *Right Place... Wrong Time*, so many of the pub regulars parted with their hard-earned cash to buy their own personal copies from me. Given my humble efforts as an author, that is a sign of true friendship.

So many people I know seem to have an ambition to publish their own life story and why shouldn't they?

I never dreamed that I would so sell very many copies of my autobiography.

While as an author I have not exactly found my way on to the bestsellers list and I never expected them to. The sales results of *Right Place…Wrong Time* left me speechless nonetheless. I honestly thought we'd be lucky to sell a hundred copies, especially in the middle of a global pandemic. I did a few radio and newspaper interviews but as my friend, the journalist Bel Mooney told me, garnering publicity to sell books is so tough if you are not exactly a household name. Perhaps if I had a few chums in Telly-land, the whole book sales process may have been considerably easier and more successful, but hey-ho.

Nursing a variety of injuries and in between undergoing surgeries as a result of a car crash on the road with a drunk-driver, I have written most of my first two books whilst propped up in bed, in between hip and knee operations. The view out of my bedroom window is hardly panoramic. When Bevvy and I first moved into the quiet village we call home back in 2009, we had a shed erected very close to our bedroom window. Much of my view is of the roof of the shed and my often-overgrown garden hedge. Sometimes the beating of the rain on the shed roof helps me relax and concentrate.

I find that the regular and mostly welcome bedroom invasions from two scampish canine villains called Stan and Ollie are quite inspiring. 'My Boys' are Old English sheepdogs and brothers who truly love each other and me as well. Together bound in and leap onto my bed, quickly moving in for doggy-lick style kisses at regular intervals, daytime and night. As a result of their love, I am never alone in my thoughts for long.

Bevvy and I travelled to South Wales to pick them up from their litter as pups. They say that dog breeds tend to pick the owners and not vice-versa. My previous boy-hound Oscar, who I dedicated my first book to, was also an Old English sheepdog. When Oscar died as a result of a cancer, he left a heart-shaped hole the size of a torpedo striking amidships.

I believe that any writer needs only a modicum of peace and order, as well as a reason to sit and write every day until the book, article, review, essay or feature is completed. As there don't seem to be too many people in the world who like me much, or are even willing to tolerate me for long, I trust dogs much more than people. I have never been attacked by a dog in my life, not even as a paper boy when I was a child. Furthermore, I firmly believe that people who cannot form a friendship or association with an animal are, generally speaking, not the type of folk whose company I crave.

In my experience relationships with so many people are often not worth the effort to cultivate or maintain. A dog gives his/her love unconditionally to those in their immediate group and I think that sentencing for those who abuse animals should be made much stiffer. I personally would nail all animal abusers to the prison walls.

In the village that I live in, in my native Yorkshire we have an ancient Saxon church. In the churchyard are the gravestones of victims of the great plague around 1660-ish. Just outside the church yard there is a set of stocks, in which the arms and legs of local miscreants were tightly fastened, while local law-abiding folk pelted them with rotten vegetables. It was a form of medieval punishment. My own believe is that those who abuse sentient creatures, such as dogs or horses should be placed in stocks and pelted with rotten produce. I can't see it happening anytime soon, but it may serve to deter some of the sadists out there, who seem to keep getting away scot free after inflicting such much cruelty and pain.

Regarding some of the dogs I have been proud to call friends, without Oscar there would have been no first book. Without Stan and Ollie, I don't think I would have found this book so easy to complete.

As I have discovered during my life, dogs work together and play together and never give up on each other. Perhaps that is where 21st-century human beings have been going wrong.

\* \*
\*

# Index

Chesterfield 75, 120, 146, 181
Child 131
Christie, Tony 111, 112, 183
City Varieties theatre 73
Cleckheaton 58
Cleethorpes 48
Clitheroe, Jimmy 73
Club & Institute Union 29, 31, 107, 179
*Club Journal* 56
*Club Review* 80
Colehan, Barney 73
Coles, Christine 122
Colleano, Bonnar 133
Colliery Houses 85
*The Comedians* 112
Conservatives 106
Cook, Phil 81
'Cook's Tour' 81
Cooper 147
Copperfield, David 160
Corpus Christi club 61
Corrigan, Jimmy 120
Cortonwood colliery 93
County Durham 93
Covid 9, 18, 133, 179
Cowell 110, 130
Craft, Mike 157
Cresters 152
Cricket, Jimmy 100
Crisco 164
Crofton 39
Cromer 113
Crompton, Colin 57, 74
Crossland, Al 163
Crossland, Neil 182
*The Cruise* 100, 109, 195
Cryne 27
Cryne, Patrick 26
Cumberland 93
Cumbria 78, 188

Currie 107

**D**

Dainty, Billy 73
Dale, Martin 75, 120, 134
Daley, Jim 82, 161
Daniels, Martin 74, 188
Daniels, Paul 74, 188, 189
Darnall 51
Dave Betton 143
Davenant church 17
Davidson, Keith 160
Davies, Glynn 132
Dawes, Johnny 134
Dawson 145, 184
Delaney, Eric 178, 179
Derby 63
Derbyshire 93, 127
Devon 113
Dialhouse club 183
Diamond Boys 133
Diamond, Bobb 133
Dick, pit pony 36
Dickens, Charles 28
Discoes 153
*Doncaster Free Press* 79
Doonican, Val 73
Dragonfly 155, 184
Duke, Robin 78
Dukes & Lee 140
Dukes, Ronnie 140
Durham, Geoffrey 131

**E**

Eagle Place 17
East End 16
East Ward labour club 67
Edwards, Lance 100
Embassy club 183
Emmerdale 160
England 27, 46, 51, 72, 78, 83, 179

*The Entertainer* magazine 80
Entertainment Agents Association 164
Erica 74
Excelsior Crisps club 63

**F**

FA Cup 26
'The Faker' 132
Falkland Islands 106
Farmers club 154
Farnworth 83
Farrell, Slim 163
Fieldhead psychiatric hospital 12
Fiesta clubs 120, 183
Fisher, Don & Stella 111
Fitzwilliam 46, 156
Fletcher, Peter 183
Foo-Foo Lamar's 75
Ford, Paul 79
'Fordi's Flyer'. 79
France, Michael 160
Francis Tumblety 16
Franks, Derek 163
Friendly Societies Act 29
Frontier club 182
*The Full Monty* 176
Fun Pubs 184
Fylde coast 51, 179

**G**

Gebhards butchers 48
General Strike of 1926 94
The Gents 132, 133, 154
Germany 33, 114, 116, 176
GLC (Greater London Council) 17
Golden Eagle pub 85
*The Good Old Days* 73
Good, Dave 60

The Talk of East Anglia 120
The Talk of the Coast 120, 187
The Talk of the North 75, 120
Tanya Tevaro & Session 181
*The Tenant of Wildfell Hall* 48
Terry, Mike 160
*That's Life* 131
Thatcher, Margaret 22, 37, 93, 94, 95, 96, 102, 104, 105, 106
Thomas, Mark 192
Thornes WMC 101
Thorpe Arch prison officers' club 116
*Three of a Kind* 160
Thurnscoe 100
Tiffany's clubs 186
'Tin Hat' club 56
Tinsley 51
Tokyo 171
Tomlin, Jim 196
*Top of the Pops* 131
Tory Party 22, 95, 107, 166
Tottenham Hotspur 47
Trafalgar Square 102
Tranter, Harry 187
TUC 96
Tumblety 16
Tunnicliffe, Trevor 134
Turfrey, Les 117
Turner, Bill 163
Two Good Reasons 59

**U**
UDM 97
UK Cabaret 78

Ullman, Tracey 160
University College London 17

**V**
Victoria 49
Victorians 18, 20, 26, 27, 28, 73
Vincent, Dick 51

**W**
Wagstaffe, John 163
*Waiting to Be Seen* 132
Wakefield 12, 19, 34, 39, 42, 48, 69, 75, 77, 99, 100, 101, 116, 117, 119, 120, 156, 184, 185, 186, 187, 188, 199
*Wakefield & District Review* 77
*Wakefield Express* 77
Wakefield market 48
Wakefield theatre club 75, 119, 120, 184, 187, 188
Wakes Weeks 51
Wales 51, 80, 93, 201
Walk & Windy 167
Walker, Peter 93
Wallis, Peter 134, 151
Watford, Pamela 80
Wayland, Derek 80
Wayne, Tony 159
Webb, Denis 78
Webster, Terry 158
West Midlands 79
West, Rudi 192
Westerton Road WMC 68
Westmoreland 93
Wetherby 116
Whale 101, 102
The Wheeltappers &

Shunters Social Club 57, 74
White, Joe 30, 38
Whitechapel 16, 17
Whitechapel Workhouse Infirmary 17
Whyte, Tony 120, 184
Wickham, Tommy 186
Wigan 62
Williams, Charlie 112
Wiltshire 29
Wincobank 51
Windsor, Jim 185
Winter, Bryan 196
Wisdom 119
Wolverhampton Wanderers 47
Wood, Victoria 131
Wood's lodging house 49
WR&P Bingley 50

**Y**
Yardley 126
York 16, 30
Yorke, Janice 122
Yorkshire 12, 19, 26, 30, 34, 36, 48, 49, 50, 51, 59, 60, 63, 70, 72, 76, 78, 79, 80, 82, 83, 85, 88, 93, 100, 101, 104, 111, 116, 126, 132, 154, 161, 162, 163, 164, 179, 186, 194, 196, 199, 201
Yorkshire Agents Association 164
Yorkshire Television 83
Young, Barry 186

**Z**
Zimbabwe 61
Zimmertones 157, 167

209

## More from this author

# RIGHT PLACE... WRONG TIME

### A Life in Northern Clubland by Mark Ritchie

*234pp | pbk | £14.99*
*ISBN: 9781908755438*

**Order at desearthearts.com also available from www.mark-ritchie.co.uk and all online/bricks & mortar bookstores.**

MARK RITCHIE delivers an autobiography which may chime with people who in their lives feel they have somehow always been in the right place but the wrong time. Mark tells an extraordinary life story with a candour which is both self-revealing and at times jarringly honest.

Although not a household name, Yorkshireman Mark is a familiar name to show business insiders for over 30 years. His career as a stand-up comedian has seen him travelling the globe performing comedy on cruise ships and international nightclubs. Since turning full-time professional back in 1983, he has worked in the steadily declining world of the northern club and cabaret scene, providing fascinating stories from the working men's clubs and holiday centres.